Mastering Search Engine Marketing: A Comprehensive Guide for Everyone

Harold Carl

Copyright © [2023]

Title: Mastering Search Engine Marketing: A Comprehensive Guide for Everyone
Author's: Harold Carl

All rights reserved. No part of this publication may be reproduced, stored in a retrieval system, or transmitted in any form or by any means, electronic, mechanical, photocopying, recording, or otherwise, without the prior written permission of the publisher or author, except in the case of brief quotations embodied in critical reviews and certain other non-commercial uses permitted by copyright law.

This book was printed and published by [Publisher's: **Harold Carl**] in [2023]

ISBN:

TABLE OF CONTENT

Chapter 1: Introduction to Search Engine Marketing   10

Understanding Search Engine Marketing

Importance of Search Engine Marketing

Evolution of Search Engine Marketing

Chapter 2: Fundamentals of Search Engine Marketing   16

Search Engine Basics

Search Engine Algorithms

Keyword Research

On-Page Optimization

Off-Page Optimization

Link Building Strategies

Chapter 3: Pay-per-Click Advertising 28

Introduction to Pay-per-Click (PPC) Advertising

Creating Effective PPC Campaigns

Keyword Selection for PPC

Ad Copywriting

Bidding Strategies

Monitoring and Optimizing PPC Campaigns

Chapter 4: Search Engine Advertising Networks 41

Google Ads

Bing Ads

Yahoo Gemini

Amazon Advertising

Social Media Advertising

Chapter 5: Search Engine Optimization (SEO)   51

SEO Techniques and Best Practices

On-Page SEO Optimization

Off-Page SEO Optimization

Local SEO Strategies

Mobile SEO Optimization

Technical SEO Considerations

Chapter 6: Content Marketing for Search Engines   63

Importance of Content Marketing in SEO

Creating High-Quality Content

Optimizing Content for Search Engines

Content Distribution and Promotion

Content Marketing Analytics

Chapter 7: Search Engine Marketing Analytics 73

Tracking and Measuring Success

Tools for Search Engine Marketing Analytics

Understanding Metrics and KPIs

Conversion Tracking and Analysis

A/B Testing and Optimization

Chapter 8: Local Search Engine Marketing 83

Local SEO Strategies for Small Businesses

Local Directory Listings and Citations

Managing Online Reviews and Reputation

Local Advertising and Promotions

Location-Based Targeting

Chapter 9: Mobile Search Engine Marketing   93

Mobile SEO Optimization Techniques

Mobile Advertising Strategies

Responsive Web Design for Mobile

Mobile App Marketing

Voice Search Optimization

Chapter 10: Advanced Search Engine Marketing Strategies   103

Remarketing and Retargeting

Video Advertising on Search Engines

International Search Engine Marketing

Influencer Marketing in Search Engine Marketing

Artificial Intelligence and Machine Learning in SEM

Chapter 11: Search Engine Marketing for E-commerce 113

E-commerce SEO Strategies

Product Listing Ads (PLA)

Shopping Campaigns

Dynamic Remarketing for E-commerce

Conversion Rate Optimization for E-commerce

Chapter 12: Future Trends in Search Engine Marketing 124

Voice Search and Virtual Assistants

Mobile-First Indexing

Personalization in Search Engine Marketing

Augmented Reality and Visual Search

Blockchain and Search Engine Marketing

Chapter 13: Ethical Considerations in Search Engine Marketing   134

Adherence to Search Engine Guidelines

Transparency in Advertising

User Privacy and Data Protection

Ethical Link Building Practices

Responsible Use of AI in SEM

Chapter 14: Conclusion and Action Plan   144

Recap of Key Concepts

Developing a Search Engine Marketing Strategy

Implementing and Monitoring the Strategy

Constant Learning and Adaptation

Resources for Further Exploration

Chapter 1: Introduction to Search Engine Marketing

Understanding Search Engine Marketing

In today's digital age, where the internet has become an integral part of our lives, search engine marketing has emerged as a powerful tool for businesses to enhance their online presence and reach their target audience effectively. In this subchapter, we will delve into the world of search engine marketing and explore its various aspects, benefits, and strategies.

Search engine marketing (SEM) refers to the practice of promoting a website by increasing its visibility on search engine result pages (SERPs) through paid advertising. It encompasses both search engine optimization (SEO) and pay-per-click (PPC) advertising, making it a comprehensive approach to maximize marketing effects and drive traffic to websites.

One of the key advantages of search engine marketing is its ability to target specific niches and audiences. Whether you are a small business owner, a marketer, or an individual looking to promote your personal brand, SEM offers a range of options to suit your unique marketing needs.

By understanding the algorithms and ranking factors used by search engines, you can optimize your website to rank higher in organic search results. This process, known as SEO, involves various techniques such as keyword research, on-page optimization, link building, and content creation. With the right SEO strategy, you can increase your website's visibility, improve its organic traffic, and ultimately boost your marketing efforts.

In addition to SEO, search engine marketing also encompasses PPC advertising. PPC allows businesses to bid on keywords relevant to their products or services and display ads on search engine result pages. This form of advertising ensures that your ads are displayed to a highly targeted audience actively searching for related information, increasing the chances of conversions and sales.

To master search engine marketing, it is crucial to familiarize yourself with popular platforms such as Google Ads, Bing Ads, and social media advertising channels. Each platform offers unique features and targeting options that can be leveraged to maximize your marketing effects.

In conclusion, understanding search engine marketing is essential for individuals and businesses alike, as it provides a comprehensive approach to enhance online visibility, target specific niches, and drive traffic to websites. By incorporating both SEO and PPC strategies, you can effectively optimize your marketing efforts, increase brand exposure, and achieve your desired marketing goals. So, get ready to dive into the world of search engine marketing and unlock its immense potential for your business or personal brand.

Importance of Search Engine Marketing

The Importance of Search Engine Marketing

In today's digital age, search engine marketing (SEM) has become a vital component of any successful marketing strategy. Whether you are a business owner, marketer, or simply interested in understanding the power of online advertising, mastering SEM is essential. This subchapter explores the significance of SEM and how it can have a profound impact on marketing efforts across various niches.

First and foremost, search engine marketing allows businesses to increase their online visibility and reach a larger audience. With billions of searches conducted on search engines like Google every day, having a strong presence in search engine results pages (SERPs) is crucial. By utilizing SEM techniques such as search engine optimization (SEO) and pay-per-click (PPC) advertising, businesses can ensure that their products or services are easily discoverable by potential customers.

Additionally, SEM provides marketers with valuable insights and data to optimize their marketing efforts. Through various tools and platforms, marketers can analyze search trends, keywords, and user behavior. This data-driven approach allows for more targeted and effective marketing campaigns, resulting in higher conversion rates and return on investment.

Moreover, SEM offers a level playing field for businesses of all sizes. Unlike traditional advertising methods, where large budgets often dominate, SEM allows even small businesses to compete with industry giants. By focusing on relevant keywords, delivering quality content, and optimizing website performance, businesses can achieve top rankings in search results, regardless of their marketing budget.

For marketers focused on specific niches, such as beauty, fashion, or technology, SEM provides an avenue to target their desired audience effectively. With advanced targeting options available in SEM platforms, marketers can tailor their ads to reach specific demographics, locations, and interests. This precision targeting ensures that marketing efforts are directed towards the most relevant audience, resulting in higher engagement and conversions.

In conclusion, search engine marketing is of utmost importance in today's digital landscape. Its ability to increase online visibility, provide valuable insights, level the playing field, and target specific niches makes it an indispensable tool for marketers across all industries. By mastering SEM techniques, businesses and marketers can stay ahead of the competition, build brand awareness, and ultimately drive revenue. Whether you are a seasoned marketer or just starting out, understanding and implementing search engine marketing strategies is critical for success in the ever-evolving world of marketing.

Evolution of Search Engine Marketing

In today's digital age, search engine marketing (SEM) has become a crucial aspect of every marketing strategy. It has revolutionized the way businesses attract customers and generate leads. The evolution of SEM has been remarkable, and understanding its journey is essential to master this powerful tool.

Search engine marketing began with the advent of search engines themselves. In the early days, businesses focused on optimizing their websites for search engines, which involved incorporating relevant keywords and meta tags. This approach, known as search engine optimization (SEO), aimed to improve organic rankings and increase visibility on search engine result pages (SERPs).

However, as more businesses started to compete for top rankings, new strategies had to be devised. This led to the birth of paid search advertising, also known as pay-per-click (PPC) advertising. Google AdWords, now Google Ads, pioneered this new advertising model, allowing businesses to bid on keywords and display their ads above organic search results.

With the rise of social media platforms, SEM expanded beyond search engines. Social media advertising became an integral part of SEM, offering businesses a new way to reach their target audience. Platforms like Facebook, Instagram, and LinkedIn allowed marketers to create highly targeted campaigns based on demographics, interests, and behavior.

The evolution of SEM did not stop there. As voice search gained popularity, marketers had to adapt their strategies to optimize for voice queries. This meant understanding how people search using voice assistants like Siri, Google Assistant, or Amazon Alexa and tailoring content accordingly.

Furthermore, the introduction of artificial intelligence (AI) and machine learning (ML) has revolutionized SEM. AI-powered algorithms now help businesses optimize their campaigns, target the right audience, and analyze data to make informed decisions. Automation tools streamline the process, saving time and resources while maximizing results.

The evolution of SEM has had a profound impact on marketing effects. It provides businesses with the ability to precisely target their audience, measure the success of campaigns, and optimize their marketing efforts in real-time. SEM has become an indispensable tool for businesses of all sizes, allowing them to compete in the ever-growing digital landscape.

As a marketer, understanding the evolution of SEM is crucial to stay ahead of the competition. This subchapter will delve into the various stages of SEM's evolution, from basic SEO techniques to advanced AI-powered strategies. Whether you are a beginner or an experienced marketer, this comprehensive guide will equip you with the knowledge and skills needed to master search engine marketing and harness its full potential for your marketing effects.

Chapter 2: Fundamentals of Search Engine Marketing

Search Engine Basics

In today's digital age, search engines have become an integral part of our daily lives. Whether you are a business owner, marketer, or simply an avid internet user, understanding the basics of search engines is crucial for maximizing marketing effects and reaching your target audience effectively. This subchapter aims to provide a comprehensive overview of search engine basics, equipping you with the knowledge to navigate this complex landscape.

To start, let's define what a search engine is. Simply put, a search engine is a software program designed to help users find information on the internet. The most popular search engine today is Google, followed by Bing and Yahoo. These search engines utilize complex algorithms to analyze websites and rank them based on relevance to the user's search query.

One key concept to grasp is the importance of search engine optimization (SEO). SEO refers to the practice of optimizing your website and content to improve its visibility in search engine results. By understanding how search engines work, you can make strategic decisions to enhance your website's ranking, driving more organic traffic and ultimately boosting your marketing effects.

Search engines use crawlers, also known as spiders or bots, to scan the internet and index web pages. When a user enters a search query, the search engine retrieves relevant pages from its index and displays them in the search engine results page (SERP). Understanding how search engines determine relevance is crucial for marketers. Factors such as keyword usage, website authority, user experience, and mobile-friendliness all play a role in search engine rankings.

Another vital aspect of search engine basics is understanding the difference between organic and paid search results. Organic results are the unpaid listings that appear based on their relevance to the user's query. In contrast, paid results, often referred to as search engine marketing (SEM) or pay-per-click (PPC) ads, are advertisements that appear at the top or bottom of the SERP. While paid ads can provide immediate visibility, organic results are generally trusted more by users and tend to have a long-term impact on marketing effects.

By mastering the basics of search engines, you can unlock a world of opportunities to enhance your marketing effects. From understanding SEO techniques to leveraging paid ads, search engine marketing is an essential tool for reaching your target audience and achieving your marketing goals. Stay tuned for the following chapters, where we will delve deeper into advanced search engine marketing strategies, empowering you to stay ahead of the competition and maximize your marketing effects.

Search Engine Algorithms

In the world of digital marketing, understanding search engine algorithms is crucial to achieving success and maximizing the impact of your marketing efforts. Search engines like Google, Bing, and Yahoo use complex algorithms to determine the relevance and ranking of websites in their search results. These algorithms are constantly evolving and becoming more sophisticated, making it essential for marketers to stay updated and adapt their strategies accordingly.

Search engine algorithms are designed to provide users with the most relevant and high-quality search results. They take into consideration a wide range of factors to determine the ranking of a webpage. Some of these factors include keyword relevance, website authority, user experience, content quality, and social signals.

Keyword relevance is a fundamental aspect of search engine algorithms. By analyzing the keywords used in a search query and comparing them to the content on various websites, search engines determine the relevance of a webpage to a user's search. Marketers need to optimize their websites with relevant keywords to increase their chances of ranking higher in search results.

Website authority is another crucial factor considered by search engine algorithms. Websites that have a strong online presence, quality backlinks, and a good reputation are more likely to rank higher. Marketers can enhance their website's authority by building high-quality backlinks, creating valuable content, and engaging with their audience through social media and other platforms.

User experience is a key focus of search engine algorithms. Websites that are user-friendly, easy to navigate, and provide valuable information tend to rank higher. Marketers should ensure that their websites are well-designed, optimized for mobile devices, and offer a seamless browsing experience to improve their rankings.

Content quality is also a significant factor in search engine algorithms. Websites with high-quality, relevant, and engaging content are more likely to rank higher. Marketers should focus on creating valuable and informative content that meets the needs of their target audience.

Social signals, such as likes, shares, and comments on social media platforms, also play a role in search engine algorithms. Search engines consider social signals as an indication of a website's popularity and relevance. Marketers should leverage social media platforms to engage with their audience and encourage social sharing to improve their rankings.

Understanding search engine algorithms and how they work is essential for marketers to maximize the impact of their marketing efforts. By optimizing websites with relevant keywords, building website authority, improving user experience, creating high-quality content, and leveraging social signals, marketers can improve their website's visibility and increase their chances of ranking higher in search results. Stay updated with the latest algorithm changes and adapt your strategies accordingly to stay ahead in the competitive world of search engine marketing.

Keyword Research

In today's digital age, where the online marketplace is becoming increasingly crowded, it is crucial for marketers to understand the importance of keyword research. This subchapter will delve into the intricacies of keyword research and how it can significantly impact marketing efforts.

Keyword research is the process of identifying and analyzing specific words and phrases that people enter into search engines when looking for information, products, or services. By understanding the search patterns and preferences of your target audience, you can optimize your marketing campaigns to align with their needs and desires.

Effective keyword research allows marketers to gain valuable insights into consumer behavior and preferences. By identifying the keywords that are most relevant to your niche, you can tailor your marketing messages to resonate with your target audience. This enables you to attract qualified leads and drive relevant traffic to your website.

There are several tools and techniques available to aid in keyword research. One popular tool is Google Keyword Planner, which provides insights into keyword search volume, competition, and related keywords. Other tools like SEMrush and Ahrefs allow marketers to conduct in-depth competitor analysis and uncover untapped keyword opportunities.

When conducting keyword research, it is essential to strike a balance between high search volume and low competition. While targeting high search volume keywords may seem tempting, it often leads to fierce competition and makes it difficult for marketers to achieve top search engine rankings. On the other hand, targeting low competition keywords may result in limited traffic. Therefore, it is crucial to find the sweet spot that aligns with your marketing objectives.

Furthermore, keyword research is an ongoing process. As consumer preferences and search trends evolve, it is imperative to continually monitor and update your keyword strategy. By staying up-to-date with the latest industry trends and regularly analyzing your keyword performance, you can ensure that your marketing efforts remain effective and relevant.

In conclusion, keyword research is a vital component of any successful marketing campaign. By understanding the search patterns and preferences of your target audience, you can optimize your marketing efforts to attract qualified leads and drive relevant traffic to your website. Utilizing tools and techniques such as Google Keyword Planner, SEMrush, and Ahrefs can provide valuable insights into keyword search volume, competition, and related keywords. Remember to strike a balance between high search volume and low competition keywords and to continually monitor and update your keyword strategy to stay ahead in the ever-evolving digital landscape.

On-Page Optimization

In the ever-evolving world of digital marketing, having a strong online presence is crucial for businesses of all sizes. One key aspect of establishing and maintaining that presence is on-page optimization. In this subchapter, we will delve into the intricacies of on-page optimization and how it can significantly impact your marketing efforts.

On-page optimization refers to the practice of optimizing various elements on your website to improve its visibility and performance in search engine results pages (SERPs). It involves making strategic changes to your website's content, meta tags, URL structure, internal linking, and more. By optimizing these on-page elements, you can enhance your website's relevancy and increase its chances of ranking higher in search engine rankings.

The first and most fundamental step in on-page optimization is keyword research. Understanding what keywords your target audience is using to search for products or services similar to yours is crucial. By incorporating these keywords naturally throughout your website's content, you can increase the chances of your website being displayed prominently in search results.

Another crucial aspect of on-page optimization is creating compelling and relevant meta tags. Meta tags, including title tags and meta descriptions, provide a brief summary of your webpage's content to search engines and potential visitors. Crafting attention-grabbing and keyword-rich meta tags can significantly improve your click-through rates and ultimately drive more organic traffic to your website.

URL structure is often an overlooked aspect of on-page optimization. A clean and concise URL structure not only helps search engines understand your website's hierarchy but also makes it more user-friendly. By incorporating relevant keywords in your URLs and making them easily readable, you can improve your website's visibility and make it more accessible to both search engines and users.

Internal linking is another powerful on-page optimization technique that can significantly impact your website's visibility. By strategically linking relevant pages within your website, you can not only improve the user experience but also distribute link equity throughout your website, helping search engines discover and index your webpages more effectively.

In conclusion, on-page optimization plays a crucial role in improving your website's visibility and overall marketing efforts. By conducting thorough keyword research, crafting compelling meta tags, optimizing your URL structure, and implementing effective internal linking strategies, you can enhance your website's relevancy, increase its organic visibility, and ultimately drive more targeted traffic to your business. Stay tuned for the next subchapter, where we will delve into the world of off-page optimization and how it can further boost your marketing efforts.

Off-Page Optimization

In the ever-evolving world of search engine marketing, it is crucial to understand the importance of off-page optimization. While on-page optimization focuses on enhancing your website's content and structure, off-page optimization involves activities that take place outside of your website, yet have a significant impact on your search engine rankings.

Off-page optimization primarily revolves around two key factors: backlinks and social signals. Backlinks are links from other websites that direct users to your site. They serve as a vote of confidence from other webmasters and search engines, indicating that your website is reputable and trustworthy. The more high-quality and relevant backlinks you have, the higher your website will rank in search engine results pages (SERPs).

Building backlinks can be achieved through various strategies. One common method is outreach, where you reach out to other website owners or bloggers in your industry and request them to include a link to your site. Guest blogging is another effective way to generate backlinks, allowing you to share your expertise with a new audience and earn a link back to your site in return.

Social signals, on the other hand, refer to the engagement and interactions your website receives on social media platforms. Search engines consider the number of likes, shares, comments, and overall social media presence as indicators of your website's popularity and authority. Therefore, it is crucial to actively engage with your audience on social media, sharing valuable content, and encouraging users to share and interact with your posts.

Additionally, off-page optimization also involves building relationships and establishing your brand's authority within your industry. This can be achieved through influencer marketing, where you collaborate with influential individuals or brands to promote your products or services. By associating your brand with recognized authorities, you not only boost your credibility but also increase the likelihood of gaining valuable backlinks and social signals.

Furthermore, off-page optimization encompasses online reputation management. Monitoring and actively managing your online reputation is essential to ensure that your brand image remains positive and trustworthy. Responding promptly and effectively to customer feedback and reviews, both positive and negative, can help build trust and establish a strong online presence.

In conclusion, off-page optimization plays a vital role in improving your website's visibility, credibility, and ultimately, your search engine rankings. By actively engaging in backlink building, social media interactions, influencer marketing, and online reputation management, you can enhance your marketing efforts and achieve long-term success in the competitive world of search engine marketing.

Link Building Strategies

In the ever-evolving world of digital marketing, link building remains a crucial component of any successful search engine marketing (SEM) strategy. A well-executed link building campaign can greatly enhance your marketing efforts and drive more traffic to your website. In this subchapter, we will delve into the various link building strategies that can help you achieve your marketing goals and maximize the impact of your SEM efforts.

1. Guest Blogging: One of the most effective link building strategies is guest blogging. By contributing high-quality content to reputable websites in your niche, you can secure valuable backlinks to your own site. This not only increases your website's visibility but also establishes you as an authority in your field.

2. Broken Link Building: Another powerful strategy is broken link building. This involves identifying broken links on relevant websites and reaching out to the webmasters to suggest replacing them with links to your own content. This win-win approach helps the website owner fix broken links while providing you with valuable backlinks.

3. Influencer Outreach: Connecting with influencers in your industry can significantly boost your link building efforts. By building relationships with influencers, you can secure guest posting opportunities, collaborations, and endorsements, leading to increased visibility and credibility for your brand.

4. Content Promotion: Creating valuable and shareable content is essential, but it is equally important to promote that content to generate backlinks. By leveraging social media, email marketing, and

online communities, you can amplify the reach of your content, increasing the likelihood of others linking to it.

5. Resource Link Building: Creating valuable resources, such as comprehensive guides, industry reports, or infographics, can attract high-quality backlinks. These resources help establish your brand as a reliable source of information, making it more likely for others to link back to your content.

6. Internal Linking: While often overlooked, internal linking is a fundamental link building strategy. By strategically linking relevant pages within your website, you not only improve user experience but also enhance your website's overall SEO performance.

Remember, link building is not about quantity, but quality. Focus on acquiring links from reputable and relevant websites to ensure long-term success. Additionally, regularly monitor and analyze your link building efforts to identify what works best for your niche and adjust your strategy accordingly.

By implementing these link building strategies, you can enhance your marketing effects, increase your website's visibility, and ultimately drive more targeted traffic to your site. Stay proactive, adapt to the ever-changing digital landscape, and continuously refine your link building efforts to stay ahead of the competition.

Chapter 3: Pay-per-Click Advertising

Introduction to Pay-per-Click (PPC) Advertising

Pay-per-Click (PPC) advertising is a powerful tool in the world of digital marketing. It allows businesses to reach their target audience effectively and efficiently, driving traffic to their websites and increasing brand visibility. In this subchapter, we will explore the fundamental concepts of PPC advertising, its benefits, and how it can be leveraged to achieve marketing effects for businesses of all sizes and niches.

PPC advertising is a model in which advertisers pay a fee each time their ad is clicked. It is commonly associated with search engine advertising, where advertisers bid on keywords relevant to their products or services. When a user searches for those keywords, the ads appear at the top or bottom of the search engine results page (SERP). The placement of these ads is determined by a combination of bid amount and quality score – a metric that evaluates the relevance and quality of the ad.

One of the primary benefits of PPC advertising is its ability to drive targeted traffic to a website. By bidding on specific keywords, businesses can ensure that their ads are shown to users actively searching for related products or services. This intent-driven approach increases the likelihood of conversions, as the users are already in the mindset of making a purchase or taking a desired action. Additionally, PPC advertising allows for precise targeting options, such as location, demographics, and device type, enabling businesses to focus their efforts on the most relevant audience.

Furthermore, PPC advertising provides instant results. Unlike organic search engine optimization (SEO) efforts, which can take months to yield significant results, PPC campaigns generate immediate visibility and traffic. This makes it an ideal marketing tool for time-sensitive promotions, product launches, or events. With the ability to control budgets and measure performance through detailed analytics, businesses can optimize their PPC campaigns in real-time, ensuring maximum return on investment (ROI).

In this subchapter, we will dive deeper into the intricacies of PPC advertising, including keyword research, campaign setup, ad creation, and optimization techniques. We will also explore different PPC platforms, such as Google Ads and Bing Ads, and discuss the importance of monitoring and analyzing campaign data to make informed decisions.

Whether you are a beginner looking to learn the basics of PPC advertising or an experienced marketer seeking to refine your strategies, this subchapter will provide you with the knowledge and tools to master the art of PPC advertising and achieve impactful marketing effects for your business.

Creating Effective PPC Campaigns

Pay-Per-Click (PPC) advertising has become an essential component of any successful marketing strategy in today's digital landscape. Whether you are a seasoned marketer or just starting out, understanding how to create effective PPC campaigns can significantly enhance your marketing efforts and drive impactful results. In this subchapter, we will delve into the key aspects of creating successful PPC campaigns and provide practical tips for maximizing your marketing effects.

1. Setting Clear Goals: Before diving into any PPC campaign, it is crucial to define your objectives. Are you aiming to increase brand awareness, drive website traffic, generate leads, or boost sales? Clearly defining your goals will help you structure your campaign effectively and measure its success.

2. Conducting Thorough Keyword Research: Keywords are the backbone of any PPC campaign. Extensive keyword research will enable you to identify relevant terms and phrases that your target audience is searching for. Utilize keyword research tools to discover high-performing keywords and build a comprehensive list to optimize your campaign.

3. Crafting Compelling Ad Copy: Your ad copy is your chance to capture the attention of your audience and entice them to click on your ad. Make sure your copy is concise, compelling, and aligned with the user's intent. Use strong call-to-action phrases to encourage click-through rates and conversions.

4. Implementing Ad Extensions: Ad extensions are additional pieces of relevant information that can be added to your ad, such as site links, call buttons, or location information. These extensions not only provide more value to your audience but also improve the visibility and performance of your ads.

5. Optimizing Landing Pages: A well-designed landing page is crucial to maximizing the effectiveness of your PPC campaign. Ensure that your landing page is relevant, visually appealing, and optimized for conversions. Streamline the user experience, highlight your unique selling proposition, and include clear call-to-action buttons to encourage desired actions.

6. Monitoring and Optimizing: PPC campaigns require constant monitoring and optimization to ensure optimal performance. Regularly analyze your campaign metrics, such as click-through rates, conversion rates, and cost per conversion. Use this data to identify areas for improvement and make data-driven adjustments.

7. A/B Testing: Experimentation is key to creating effective PPC campaigns. Conduct A/B tests with different ad copies, keywords, landing pages, or targeting options to identify what works best for your audience. Continuously refine and optimize your campaigns based on the insights gained from these tests.

By following these steps, you can create highly effective PPC campaigns that drive tangible marketing effects. However, it's important to remember that PPC advertising is an ongoing process that requires continuous refinement and adaptation. Stay up-to-date with industry trends, experiment with new strategies, and continually refine your campaigns to stay ahead of the competition and maximize your marketing efforts.

Keyword Selection for PPC

In the fast-paced world of digital marketing, Pay-Per-Click (PPC) advertising has become a vital tool for businesses to reach their target audience and drive traffic to their websites. However, to ensure the success of your PPC campaigns, one crucial step is often overlooked – keyword selection.

Keywords are the foundation of any PPC campaign. They are the words or phrases that potential customers use when searching for products or services online. The right keywords can attract highly relevant traffic to your website, increasing the chances of conversions and maximizing your marketing efforts.

When selecting keywords for your PPC campaigns, it is essential to consider both relevance and search volume. Relevance refers to how closely a keyword aligns with your business and the products or services you offer. Choosing relevant keywords ensures that your ads are shown to the right audience, increasing the likelihood of attracting qualified leads.

On the other hand, search volume refers to the number of searches conducted for a particular keyword. While high search volume keywords may seem attractive, they often come with fierce competition. It is crucial to strike a balance between relevance and search volume, focusing on a mix of high-relevance, high-search-volume keywords, and long-tail keywords – more specific phrases that may have lower search volume but higher conversion rates.

To determine the best keywords for your PPC campaigns, you can utilize various tools and techniques. Start by brainstorming a list of keywords that are relevant to your business and the marketing effects you wish to achieve. Then, use keyword research tools such as Google Keyword Planner, SEMrush, or Moz's Keyword Explorer to gather data on search volume, competition, and related keywords.

Once you have compiled a list of potential keywords, it is crucial to continually monitor their performance and make adjustments as necessary. PPC campaigns require ongoing optimization, and keyword selection is an ongoing process. Analyze data such as click-through rates, conversion rates, and cost-per-click to identify which keywords are driving the most valuable traffic and adjust your campaign accordingly.

In conclusion, keyword selection is a critical aspect of PPC advertising. By choosing relevant and high-performing keywords, you can attract the right audience, increase conversions, and maximize your marketing efforts. Remember to strike a balance between relevance and search volume, continuously monitor and optimize your campaigns, and stay up-to-date with the latest keyword trends in your niche. With a well-executed keyword strategy, you can master the art of PPC advertising and achieve your marketing goals.

Ad Copywriting

In the fast-paced world of digital marketing, ad copywriting plays a crucial role in capturing the attention of your target audience and driving results. Whether you are a seasoned marketer or just starting out, understanding the art of ad copywriting is essential to create compelling and persuasive advertising campaigns. This subchapter will delve into the key principles and strategies to master the art of ad copywriting.

First and foremost, it is important to understand the power of words in marketing. Your ad copy should be concise, yet impactful. Every word counts, so make sure to choose your language wisely. Craft a headline that grabs attention and conveys the key benefit or value proposition of your product or service. Remember, you only have a few seconds to capture the interest of your audience, so make it count!

Another crucial aspect of ad copywriting is understanding your target audience. Knowing their needs, desires, and pain points will help you tailor your message to resonate with them. Put yourself in their shoes and think about what would compel them to take action. By addressing their specific needs, you can create a sense of urgency and drive conversions.

Using emotional triggers in your ad copy can also be highly effective. People make decisions based on emotions, so evoke feelings of happiness, fear of missing out, or the desire for a better life. Incorporating storytelling techniques can help create a connection with your audience and make your ad more relatable.

Furthermore, incorporating social proof in your ad copy can significantly boost your credibility. Highlight positive reviews, testimonials, or case studies to demonstrate the value and trustworthiness of your product or service. People are more likely to take action if they see others have had a positive experience.

Lastly, don't forget to include a strong call-to-action (CTA) in your ad copy. Clearly instruct your audience on what action they should take next, whether it's making a purchase, signing up for a newsletter, or contacting your business. A compelling CTA can make all the difference in driving conversions.

In conclusion, ad copywriting is a skill that can greatly impact the success of your marketing efforts. By crafting persuasive and compelling ad copy, you can capture the attention of your target audience, drive engagement, and ultimately achieve your marketing goals. So, take the time to understand the principles and strategies discussed in this subchapter and unleash the power of effective ad copywriting in your marketing campaigns.

Bidding Strategies

In the ever-evolving world of search engine marketing (SEM), understanding effective bidding strategies is crucial to achieving optimal marketing results. Whether you are a business owner, marketer, or someone interested in the field of marketing effects, this subchapter will provide you with comprehensive insights into bidding strategies that can help you master the art of SEM.

When it comes to SEM, bidding plays a vital role in determining the visibility and success of your online advertising campaigns. Bidding refers to the process of placing a monetary value on the keywords or phrases you want your ads to appear for in search engine results. A well-crafted bidding strategy can ensure that your ads are shown to the right audience at the right time, maximizing your marketing efforts.

There are several bidding strategies to consider, each with its own advantages and applications:

1. Cost-per-click (CPC) Bidding: This strategy involves paying for each click generated by your ad. CPC bidding allows you to control costs while ensuring that you only pay when someone interacts with your ad, such as visiting your website or making a purchase.

2. Cost-per-thousand-impressions (CPM) Bidding: With CPM bidding, you pay a set amount for every thousand times your ad is displayed, regardless of whether users click on it. This strategy is useful for increasing brand exposure and awareness.

3. Conversion-based Bidding: This advanced strategy focuses on maximizing conversions rather than clicks or impressions. By tracking

and analyzing user behavior, you can bid more aggressively on keywords that are more likely to drive conversions, such as purchases or sign-ups.

4. Automated Bidding: Utilizing machine learning algorithms, automated bidding strategies leverage historical data and real-time signals to adjust bids automatically. These strategies help optimize performance, save time, and improve ROI.

When implementing bidding strategies, it is essential to constantly monitor and optimize your campaigns. Regularly review performance metrics such as click-through rates, conversion rates, and return on ad spend to identify areas for improvement. Adjust your bids based on the performance of specific keywords or ad groups, and conduct split testing to determine the most effective bidding strategies for your marketing objectives.

In conclusion, mastering bidding strategies is a crucial element of successful search engine marketing. By understanding the various bidding options available and constantly monitoring and optimizing your campaigns, you can ensure that your marketing efforts are not only visible but also effective in driving desired results. Stay informed and adaptable in this dynamic field to stay ahead of the competition and achieve marketing success.

Monitoring and Optimizing PPC Campaigns

In the ever-evolving world of digital marketing, Pay-Per-Click (PPC) campaigns have emerged as a powerful tool for businesses to promote their products and services online. However, simply launching a PPC campaign is not enough to guarantee success. To truly harness the potential of PPC advertising, it is imperative to monitor and optimize your campaigns consistently. In this subchapter, we will delve into the essential aspects of monitoring and optimizing PPC campaigns, equipping you with the knowledge to maximize your marketing efforts.

Monitoring your PPC campaigns is crucial for maintaining a pulse on their performance. By regularly tracking key metrics such as click-through rates, conversion rates, and cost per click, you can gain valuable insights into the effectiveness of your ads. This data provides a comprehensive overview of your campaign's strengths and weaknesses, enabling you to make informed decisions about where to allocate your budget and resources. Additionally, monitoring allows you to identify any issues or discrepancies that may arise, such as low-quality traffic or ad fatigue, so that you can promptly address them before they impact your campaign's performance.

Optimizing your PPC campaigns involves fine-tuning various elements to improve their effectiveness. One crucial aspect of optimization is keyword research. By identifying the most relevant and high-performing keywords for your business, you can ensure that your ads are reaching the right audience and generating quality leads. Furthermore, continuously optimizing your ad copy and landing pages helps increase click-through rates and conversions. A compelling ad copy combined with a well-designed landing page can significantly enhance the user experience, leading to higher engagement and improved campaign performance.

Another essential component of optimization is A/B testing. By creating multiple variations of your ads, landing pages, or even calls-to-action, you can experiment and compare their performance to determine which elements are resonating best with your target audience. This iterative approach allows you to refine and optimize your campaigns over time, ultimately driving better results and maximizing your marketing efforts.

In conclusion, monitoring and optimizing PPC campaigns are vital for achieving marketing success. By consistently monitoring key metrics and leveraging data-driven insights, you can identify areas of improvement and take proactive steps to optimize your campaigns. With a strategic approach to keyword research, ad copy, landing pages, and A/B testing, you can continually refine your PPC campaigns, enhancing their performance and maximizing your marketing ROI.

Chapter 4: Search Engine Advertising Networks

Google Ads

In today's digital age, marketing has become an integral part of every business's success. Companies are constantly striving to get their products and services noticed in an increasingly competitive market. One effective way to achieve this is through search engine marketing, and at the forefront of this strategy is Google Ads.

Google Ads is a powerful advertising platform that enables businesses to promote their offerings to a wide audience online. With over 3.5 billion searches conducted on Google each day, it provides an unparalleled opportunity to reach potential customers at the precise moment they are searching for relevant information.

This subchapter dives into the world of Google Ads, offering a comprehensive guide for everyone interested in leveraging this platform for marketing effects. Whether you are a small business owner, a marketing professional, or an aspiring digital marketer, understanding the ins and outs of Google Ads can significantly enhance your marketing efforts.

The chapter begins by outlining the fundamentals of Google Ads, providing readers with a solid foundation to build upon. It explains how the platform works, the different ad formats available, and the key metrics to track for measuring success. It also explores the various targeting options, allowing advertisers to tailor their campaigns to specific demographics, locations, or interests.

Next, the subchapter delves into the process of creating effective Google Ads campaigns. It covers keyword research, ad copywriting, and landing page optimization, equipping readers with the necessary skills to craft compelling advertisements that drive conversions. Additionally, it offers insights into ad testing and optimization techniques to continually refine and improve campaign performance.

Furthermore, this subchapter explores advanced strategies for maximizing the impact of Google Ads. It discusses remarketing, which allows businesses to re-engage with previous website visitors, and showcases the power of ad extensions to enhance the visibility and click-through rates of ads. It also touches upon the importance of tracking and analytics, emphasizing the significance of data-driven decision-making in achieving marketing objectives.

By the end of this subchapter, readers will have gained a comprehensive understanding of Google Ads and its potential for marketing effects. They will be equipped with the knowledge and skills to create and optimize successful campaigns that drive traffic, increase brand awareness, and generate conversions. Whether you are a novice or an experienced marketer, harness the power of Google Ads and take your marketing efforts to new heights.

Bing Ads

In today's digital age, search engine marketing has become an essential tool for businesses to boost their online presence and drive targeted traffic to their websites. While Google Ads may be the most popular choice for many marketers, it is important not to overlook the potential of Bing Ads. In this subchapter, we will explore the world of Bing Ads and how they can have a significant impact on your marketing efforts.

Bing Ads, the advertising platform developed by Microsoft, offers a unique opportunity to reach a diverse audience and expand your marketing reach. With Bing being the default search engine for Microsoft's Windows operating system, it is estimated that Bing Ads can reach up to 63 million searchers that are not reached by Google Ads alone. This presents a huge untapped market for businesses looking to gain a competitive advantage.

One of the key advantages of Bing Ads is its lower competition compared to Google Ads. Due to Google's dominance in the search engine market, many businesses focus their advertising efforts solely on Google Ads. This means that Bing Ads often have lower bid prices and less competition for keywords, allowing you to potentially achieve higher ad rankings at a lower cost.

Another unique feature of Bing Ads is its audience demographics. Bing users tend to be older, more affluent, and often have a higher purchasing power compared to Google users. This makes Bing Ads particularly effective for businesses targeting specific niches, such as luxury goods, financial services, or professional services.

To get started with Bing Ads, you will need to create a Microsoft Advertising account. The platform offers a user-friendly interface similar to Google Ads, making it easy to set up and manage your campaigns. You can choose from various ad formats, including text ads, shopping ads, and even video ads, to tailor your marketing message to the Bing audience.

Additionally, Bing Ads provides robust targeting options to ensure your ads are shown to the right audience. You can target based on location, language, device, and even specific demographics. This level of granularity allows you to optimize your campaigns and maximize your marketing effects.

In conclusion, Bing Ads should not be overlooked when it comes to search engine marketing. With its potential to reach a unique audience, lower competition, and powerful targeting options, Bing Ads can be a valuable addition to your marketing strategy. By mastering Bing Ads, you can unlock new opportunities and enhance your overall marketing efforts, driving more traffic and conversions to your business.

Yahoo Gemini

Yahoo Gemini is a powerful tool in the world of search engine marketing that has the potential to revolutionize your marketing efforts. In this subchapter, we will explore the ins and outs of Yahoo Gemini and how it can have a profound impact on your marketing strategy, regardless of your niche.

Yahoo Gemini is a native advertising platform that combines the power of search and native ads to deliver highly targeted and effective marketing campaigns. It allows advertisers to reach their target audience on Yahoo's search engine and network of partner sites, ensuring maximum visibility and engagement.

One of the key advantages of Yahoo Gemini is its ability to deliver ads in a native format. Native ads seamlessly blend in with the content on the page, making them less intrusive and more likely to be viewed and clicked on by users. This integration creates a positive user experience, leading to higher engagement and conversion rates.

Another significant feature of Yahoo Gemini is its precise targeting capabilities. With advanced demographic, geographic, and interest-based targeting options, advertisers can reach the right audience at the right time. This level of precision ensures that your marketing efforts are not wasted on irrelevant audiences, resulting in a higher return on investment.

Yahoo Gemini also offers robust analytics and reporting features that provide valuable insights into campaign performance. These insights allow marketers to fine-tune their campaigns, optimize their strategy, and make data-driven decisions to maximize marketing effects.

Regardless of your niche, Yahoo Gemini can help you achieve your marketing goals. Whether you are looking to increase brand awareness, drive website traffic, or boost sales, this platform has the tools and capabilities to make it happen. By leveraging the power of native advertising, precise targeting, and insightful analytics, Yahoo Gemini can take your marketing efforts to new heights.

In conclusion, Yahoo Gemini is a game-changer in the field of search engine marketing. Its native advertising capabilities, precise targeting options, and robust analytics make it an indispensable tool for marketers across all niches. If you want to master search engine marketing and achieve remarkable marketing effects, don't overlook the potential of Yahoo Gemini.

Amazon Advertising

In today's digital world, advertising plays a crucial role in the success of any marketing campaign. With the rise of e-commerce, Amazon has emerged as a dominant player in the online retail space and has revolutionized the way we shop. As a result, Amazon Advertising has become an integral part of any comprehensive marketing strategy.

Amazon Advertising is a powerful tool that allows businesses to promote their products and reach millions of potential customers. With over 300 million active customers worldwide, Amazon provides an unprecedented opportunity to connect with a vast audience. Whether you're a small business owner or a seasoned marketer, understanding Amazon Advertising is essential for maximizing your marketing effects.

One of the key advantages of Amazon Advertising is its ability to target specific audiences. Through advanced targeting options, businesses can reach customers who are actively searching for products similar to theirs. By leveraging Amazon's vast database of customer behavior and purchase history, advertisers can create highly targeted campaigns that yield better results. This level of precision targeting ensures that your ads are seen by the right people, at the right time, increasing the chances of conversion.

Another benefit of Amazon Advertising is its seamless integration with Amazon's e-commerce platform. When users search for products on Amazon, they are presented with sponsored ads that are relevant to their search queries. This native advertising format ensures that your products are displayed in a non-intrusive manner, increasing the likelihood of engagement.

Furthermore, Amazon Advertising provides valuable insights and analytics that can help businesses optimize their campaigns. By monitoring key metrics such as click-through rates, conversion rates, and return on ad spend, marketers can make data-driven decisions and refine their strategies for better results. This iterative approach allows businesses to continuously improve their advertising efforts, maximizing their marketing effects.

In conclusion, Amazon Advertising is a powerful tool that allows businesses to reach a vast audience and drive sales. Its advanced targeting options, seamless integration with the e-commerce platform, and valuable analytics make it an essential component of any comprehensive marketing strategy. Whether you're a small business owner or a seasoned marketer, mastering Amazon Advertising is crucial for maximizing your marketing effects in the ever-growing digital landscape.

Social Media Advertising

In today's digital age, social media has become an integral part of our daily lives. We use it to connect with friends and family, share updates about our lives, and even stay updated with current events. However, social media is not just a platform for personal use; it has also emerged as a powerful tool for businesses to reach their target audience. This subchapter will delve into the concept of social media advertising and its profound impact on marketing efforts.

Social media advertising refers to the process of promoting products or services through various social media platforms such as Facebook, Instagram, Twitter, and LinkedIn. With billions of active users worldwide, these platforms provide businesses with a unique opportunity to target specific demographics and engage with potential customers.

One of the key advantages of social media advertising is its ability to reach a vast audience at a relatively low cost. Traditional forms of advertising, such as television or print ads, can be expensive and may not have the same level of targeting capabilities. Social media platforms, on the other hand, allow businesses to define their target audience based on demographics, interests, and behaviors. This level of precision ensures that the advertisement reaches the right people, increasing the chances of conversion.

Moreover, social media advertising offers a range of ad formats, including image ads, video ads, carousel ads, and sponsored content, allowing businesses to choose the most suitable format for their marketing message. These formats enable businesses to showcase their products or services creatively, capturing the attention of users scrolling through their social media feeds.

Another significant advantage of social media advertising is the ability to measure and analyze campaign performance. Platforms like Facebook and Instagram provide detailed insights into the reach, engagement, and conversion rates of advertisements. This data is invaluable for marketers, as it allows them to refine their targeting strategies and optimize their campaigns for maximum effectiveness.

However, it is crucial to note that social media advertising is not a one-size-fits-all solution. Different platforms attract different user demographics, and businesses must carefully select the platforms that align with their target audience. Additionally, creating compelling and relevant content is essential to stand out in the crowded digital space.

In conclusion, social media advertising has revolutionized the marketing landscape, offering businesses a cost-effective and highly targeted way to reach their desired audience. By leveraging the power of social media platforms, businesses can amplify their brand presence, drive traffic to their websites, and ultimately boost their sales.

Chapter 5: Search Engine Optimization (SEO)

SEO Techniques and Best Practices

In today's digital age, having a strong online presence is crucial for businesses of all sizes. Search Engine Optimization (SEO) plays a vital role in ensuring that your website ranks high in search engine results pages (SERPs), driving organic traffic and boosting marketing efforts. This subchapter explores the various SEO techniques and best practices that can help you master search engine marketing, regardless of your background or industry.

Understanding the intricacies of SEO can be overwhelming, but fear not! This subchapter aims to break it down into manageable steps and provide practical insights for everyone, regardless of their marketing experience. Whether you are a small business owner, a marketing professional, or simply curious about the effects of SEO, this section has got you covered.

We begin by demystifying the core concepts of SEO, including keywords, on-page optimization, and link building. We delve into the importance of conducting comprehensive keyword research and guide you through the process of optimizing your website's content to ensure it aligns with search engine algorithms.

Furthermore, we explore the significance of user experience (UX) in SEO and how to optimize your website's design and functionality to enhance user satisfaction. From mobile responsiveness to site speed, we provide actionable tips to improve your website's performance and increase its visibility in search results.

Additionally, we tackle the ever-evolving landscape of SEO and discuss the latest trends and best practices. We explore the impact of voice search, mobile-first indexing, and the rise of artificial intelligence on SEO strategies. By staying updated with the latest trends, you can adapt your marketing efforts effectively and ensure your website remains competitive in the ever-changing digital landscape.

Lastly, we emphasize the importance of monitoring and measuring the success of your SEO efforts. We introduce various analytics tools and techniques that can help you track your website's performance, identify areas for improvement, and make data-driven decisions to optimize your marketing efforts.

Whether you are a seasoned marketer or a beginner in the field, mastering SEO techniques and best practices is essential for achieving marketing effects. This subchapter equips you with the necessary knowledge and tools to navigate the complex world of search engine marketing, helping you drive organic traffic, increase conversions, and stay ahead of the competition.

On-Page SEO Optimization

In today's digital age, having a strong online presence is crucial for businesses of all sizes. With countless websites competing for attention, it's essential to employ effective strategies to ensure your website stands out from the crowd. One such strategy is On-Page SEO Optimization, which focuses on optimizing various elements within your web pages to improve search engine rankings and drive organic traffic.

On-Page SEO Optimization is the process of optimizing individual web pages to make them more search engine friendly. By implementing certain techniques, you can enhance your website's visibility and increase its chances of appearing on the first page of search engine results. In this subchapter, we will explore the key aspects of On-Page SEO Optimization that will help you master search engine marketing and achieve outstanding marketing effects.

Firstly, we will delve into the importance of keyword research. Keywords are the foundation of any successful SEO strategy. By conducting thorough keyword research, you can identify the most relevant and highly searched terms for your niche. Integrating these keywords strategically throughout your web pages, including in titles, headings, meta descriptions, and content, will signal search engines that your website is a relevant resource for those searching for specific information.

Next, we will discuss the significance of high-quality content. Search engines prioritize websites that provide valuable and engaging content to users. By creating informative, well-written, and unique content, you can establish yourself as an authority in your industry and attract more organic traffic. Additionally, we will explore the importance of optimizing your content with relevant multimedia elements, such as images, videos, and infographics, to enhance user experience and increase the chances of your content being shared across various platforms.

Furthermore, we will address the importance of optimizing your website's structure and navigation. A well-organized and user-friendly website structure not only allows visitors to find information quickly but also helps search engines crawl and index your pages more efficiently. We will discuss techniques such as creating XML sitemaps, optimizing URL structure, and implementing breadcrumb navigation to enhance your website's overall SEO performance.

Lastly, we will touch on the significance of technical SEO elements, such as page loading speed, mobile responsiveness, and secure HTTPS connections. Search engines prioritize websites that provide a seamless user experience across different devices and ensure user data security. By optimizing these technical aspects, you can improve your website's rankings and provide an optimal browsing experience for your visitors.

By mastering the art of On-Page SEO Optimization, you can significantly improve your website's visibility, drive organic traffic, and achieve remarkable marketing effects. Whether you are a business owner, marketing professional, or simply someone interested in enhancing their online presence, the knowledge and techniques shared in this subchapter will empower you to take your search engine marketing efforts to new heights.

Off-Page SEO Optimization

In today's digital landscape, having a well-optimized website is crucial for any business looking to succeed online. While on-page SEO focuses on optimizing the content and structure of a website, off-page SEO optimization refers to the strategies employed outside of the website to improve its search engine rankings. These techniques are aimed at increasing the website's visibility, authority, and credibility across the internet. In this subchapter, we will delve into the world of off-page SEO optimization and explore the various strategies that can be employed for maximum marketing effects.

Link building is one of the most significant aspects of off-page SEO optimization. By acquiring high-quality backlinks from reputable websites, you can signal to search engines that your website is trustworthy and relevant. We will discuss the different methods of link building, such as guest posting, influencer outreach, and content syndication. Additionally, we will explore the importance of anchor text diversity and the potential risks of unethical link building practices.

Social media plays a vital role in off-page SEO optimization as well. Engaging with your audience on platforms like Facebook, Twitter, and Instagram not only helps build brand awareness but also generates social signals that search engines take into account when ranking websites. We will explore the best practices for social media engagement, including creating shareable content, leveraging user-generated content, and optimizing social media profiles.

Online reputation management is another crucial aspect of off-page SEO optimization. Positive online reviews and testimonials can greatly enhance your website's credibility and influence potential customers. We will discuss strategies for managing and improving online reputation, such as encouraging customers to leave reviews, responding to feedback promptly, and addressing negative reviews professionally.

Furthermore, we will cover the importance of local SEO optimization for businesses targeting specific geographical areas. Techniques like creating and optimizing Google My Business profiles, building local citations, and leveraging online directories can significantly enhance your website's visibility in local search results.

By implementing these off-page SEO optimization strategies, you can improve your website's rankings, increase organic traffic, and ultimately drive more conversions. Whether you are a small business owner, a marketing professional, or simply someone interested in learning about search engine marketing, this subchapter will provide you with the knowledge and tools to master off-page SEO optimization and achieve marketing effects that can propel your online success.

Local SEO Strategies

Local SEO (Search Engine Optimization) is a crucial aspect of marketing for businesses that rely on local customers. It involves optimizing a website's visibility in search engine results pages (SERPs) for location-specific searches. In this subchapter, we will explore effective local SEO strategies that can help businesses maximize their online presence and attract more local customers.

First and foremost, it is essential to claim and optimize your Google My Business (GMB) listing. This free tool from Google allows businesses to manage their online presence and appear in local search results. By providing accurate and up-to-date information, such as your business name, address, phone number, and business hours, you can improve your chances of appearing in local searches.

Another effective strategy is to optimize your website for local keywords. Conduct keyword research to identify the most relevant and frequently searched terms in your local area. Incorporate these keywords naturally into your website's content, meta tags, and headings. This will increase your website's visibility in local search results.

Creating location-specific landing pages can also boost your local SEO efforts. These pages should provide valuable and relevant content to local customers, including information about your products or services, customer reviews, and testimonials. Additionally, including a Google Map on your landing page can enhance your local SEO by showing your business location and making it easier for customers to find you.

Customer reviews play a crucial role in local SEO. Encourage satisfied customers to leave reviews on platforms like Google, Yelp, and Facebook. Positive reviews not only improve your online reputation but also contribute to higher rankings in local search results.

Local citations are mentions of your business on other websites, such as online directories, review sites, and local business associations. Ensure that your business name, address, and phone number (NAP) are consistent across all citations. This consistency helps search engines associate your business with a specific location, improving your local search rankings.

Finally, don't forget to leverage social media for local SEO. Engage with local customers by sharing local news, events, and promotions on platforms like Facebook, Instagram, and Twitter. This will not only increase your online visibility but also help establish your business as a trusted and active member of the local community.

In conclusion, implementing effective local SEO strategies is essential for businesses looking to attract more local customers. By optimizing your website, claiming your Google My Business listing, encouraging customer reviews, and leveraging social media, you can improve your online visibility and gain a competitive edge in your local market.

Mobile SEO Optimization

In today's digital age, where the majority of people access the internet through their mobile devices, it has become imperative for businesses to optimize their websites for mobile search engines. Mobile SEO optimization is the process of making your website mobile-friendly and ensuring it ranks high on mobile search engine results pages (SERPs). This subchapter will delve into the importance of mobile SEO optimization and provide valuable insights for marketing professionals and anyone interested in maximizing their online presence.

Mobile SEO optimization is crucial for several reasons. Firstly, search engines prioritize mobile-friendly websites in their rankings. With Google's mobile-first indexing, websites that are optimized for mobile devices receive higher visibility in search results. This directly impacts a website's organic traffic and its overall marketing effectiveness.

Furthermore, the majority of internet users now browse the web on their smartphones or tablets. If your website is not mobile-friendly, visitors will have a poor user experience, leading to high bounce rates and low conversion rates. This can significantly impact your marketing efforts and hinder your ability to reach and engage your target audience effectively.

To optimize your website for mobile search engines, several factors must be considered. One key aspect is responsive web design. This involves creating a website that automatically adjusts its layout, content, and functionality based on the device being used. By implementing responsive design, you ensure that your website provides a seamless user experience across all devices, whether it be a smartphone, tablet, or desktop.

Additionally, optimizing page load speed is essential for mobile SEO. Mobile users expect fast-loading websites, and search engines take this into account when ranking websites. By optimizing images, minimizing code, and utilizing caching techniques, you can significantly improve your website's loading time, resulting in a better user experience and higher search engine rankings.

Another critical aspect of mobile SEO optimization is local search optimization. Mobile users often conduct searches related to their immediate surroundings, such as "restaurants near me" or "stores nearby." By optimizing your website for local search, including incorporating location-specific keywords and ensuring your business information is accurate and up-to-date, you can increase your visibility in local search results and attract more local customers.

In conclusion, mobile SEO optimization plays a vital role in today's digital marketing landscape. By ensuring your website is mobile-friendly, loads quickly, and is optimized for local search, you can enhance your online presence and reach a wider audience. Implementing these mobile SEO strategies will not only improve your website's visibility and user experience but also have a positive impact on your marketing efforts, ultimately leading to increased brand awareness, higher organic traffic, and improved conversion rates.

Technical SEO Considerations

In today's digital age, search engine optimization (SEO) has become an integral part of any successful marketing strategy. It is crucial to ensure that your website is easily discoverable and ranks high on search engine result pages (SERPs). While there are various aspects to consider when it comes to optimizing your website for search engines, one of the most critical elements is technical SEO. In this subchapter, we will explore the technical SEO considerations that can have a significant impact on your marketing efforts.

Technical SEO refers to the optimization of your website's technical infrastructure to enhance its visibility and crawlability for search engines. It involves making necessary changes to your website's backend, such as improving website speed, optimizing mobile responsiveness, and enhancing website security. By addressing these technical aspects, you can improve your website's overall performance and subsequently boost your marketing efforts.

One of the primary technical SEO considerations is website speed. Search engines prioritize websites that offer a fast and seamless user experience. Slow-loading websites not only frustrate users but can also lead to higher bounce rates and lower rankings. Therefore, it is crucial to optimize your website's loading speed by compressing images, minifying code, and leveraging browser caching.

Another essential consideration is mobile responsiveness. With the growing number of mobile users, search engines now prioritize mobile-friendly websites. Ensuring that your website is optimized for mobile devices is crucial for improving your search engine rankings and reaching a wider audience.

Additionally, website security plays a vital role in technical SEO. Search engines prioritize secure websites to protect users from potential cyber threats. Implementing HTTPS encryption, regularly updating software, and using strong passwords are some of the measures you can take to improve your website's security and gain search engine trust.

Furthermore, optimizing your website's structure and navigation is crucial for search engine crawlers to understand and index your content effectively. Creating a logical site structure, using proper heading tags, and implementing XML sitemaps are some of the techniques that can enhance your website's crawlability.

In conclusion, technical SEO considerations are vital for anyone involved in marketing efforts. By optimizing your website's technical elements, you can improve its visibility, rankings, and overall performance. From website speed to mobile responsiveness and website security, paying attention to these factors will positively impact your marketing efforts and help you reach a broader audience.

Chapter 6: Content Marketing for Search Engines

Importance of Content Marketing in SEO

In today's digital age, where competition is fierce and the online landscape is constantly evolving, mastering search engine marketing has become crucial for every marketer. One of the most effective strategies to gain visibility and drive organic traffic to your website is through content marketing. In this subchapter, we will explore the importance of content marketing in SEO and how it can have a profound impact on your marketing efforts.

First and foremost, content marketing plays a pivotal role in improving your website's search engine optimization (SEO) rankings. Search engines like Google value high-quality, relevant, and fresh content. By consistently creating and publishing valuable content, you not only provide value to your target audience but also signal search engines that your website is a reliable and authoritative source of information. This, in turn, helps to improve your website's visibility in search engine results pages (SERPs).

Moreover, content marketing helps to establish your brand's credibility and expertise in your niche. By creating educational and informative content that addresses the pain points of your audience, you position yourself as a thought leader and gain trust from your potential customers. This trust translates into increased brand loyalty and customer retention, as well as attracting new customers who are drawn to your valuable content.

Another significant advantage of content marketing in SEO is its ability to drive organic traffic. When you create content that is optimized for relevant keywords and provides value to users, search engines are more likely to rank your website higher in search results. This increased visibility leads to more organic traffic, as users trust organic search results more than paid advertisements. By leveraging content marketing, you can tap into this valuable source of traffic and generate more leads and conversions for your business.

Furthermore, content marketing allows you to engage with your audience on various channels and platforms. By creating shareable content, you encourage your audience to spread the word about your brand, thus expanding your reach and attracting new customers. Additionally, through content marketing, you can leverage social media platforms to amplify your content's reach and engage with your audience directly.

In conclusion, content marketing is an integral part of any successful SEO strategy. It not only improves your website's visibility in search engine results but also establishes your brand's credibility, drives organic traffic, and enables you to engage with your target audience effectively. By mastering content marketing, you can unlock the full potential of search engine marketing and achieve remarkable marketing effects for your business.

Creating High-Quality Content

In the ever-evolving world of search engine marketing, one thing remains constant: the importance of high-quality content. Whether you are a seasoned marketer or just starting out, understanding how to create compelling and valuable content is crucial for achieving success in the digital landscape. This subchapter will delve into the key principles and strategies behind creating high-quality content that effectively impacts marketing efforts.

First and foremost, high-quality content should be relevant and valuable to your target audience. It should address their needs, answer their questions, and provide them with valuable insights or solutions. Conduct thorough research to understand your audience's preferences, pain points, and desires. This will help you tailor your content to meet their expectations and establish yourself as a trusted source of information.

Additionally, high-quality content should be original and unique. Avoid duplicating content from other sources, as search engines prioritize originality. Your content should bring a fresh perspective or provide a unique take on a particular topic. This will not only attract and engage your audience but also enhance your credibility and authority in the industry.

Furthermore, high-quality content should be well-structured and easy to consume. Use clear headings, subheadings, and bullet points to break down your content into digestible chunks. Incorporate relevant images, videos, or infographics to enhance the visual appeal and engage your audience further. Remember to optimize your content for mobile devices, as an increasing number of users access the internet through smartphones and tablets.

Another crucial aspect of high-quality content is its search engine optimization (SEO) strategy. Conduct keyword research to identify relevant keywords and incorporate them naturally throughout your content. Pay attention to on-page elements such as meta titles, descriptions, and alt tags to enhance your content's visibility in search engine results.

Lastly, high-quality content should be regularly updated and refreshed. As marketing trends and consumer preferences evolve, it is essential to keep your content up to date. Regularly review and update your existing content, repurpose it into different formats, or create entirely new content to stay relevant and maintain your audience's interest.

In conclusion, creating high-quality content is a fundamental pillar of effective search engine marketing. By understanding your audience, providing valuable insights, being original, optimizing for search engines, and keeping your content up to date, you can create content that not only attracts and engages your target audience but also drives successful marketing outcomes. Remember, high-quality content is the key to standing out in the competitive digital landscape and establishing your brand as a trusted authority.

Optimizing Content for Search Engines

In today's digital age, search engines have become the go-to tool for millions of people looking for information, products, and services. As a marketer, it is crucial to understand how to optimize your content for search engines in order to maximize its visibility and reach. This subchapter will delve into the various strategies and techniques that can help you achieve higher rankings and attract more organic traffic to your website.

One of the first steps in optimizing content for search engines is conducting thorough keyword research. Keywords are the foundation of search engine optimization (SEO) and play a vital role in helping search engines understand the relevance of your content. By identifying the right keywords and integrating them naturally into your content, you can improve your chances of ranking higher in search engine results pages (SERPs).

Another important aspect of optimizing content is ensuring it is user-friendly and easily accessible. Search engines prioritize websites that offer a seamless user experience, so it is crucial to have a well-structured website with clear navigation and mobile responsiveness. Additionally, optimizing your website's loading speed can significantly impact your search engine rankings.

Creating high-quality, engaging, and informative content is also key to optimizing for search engines. Search engines are constantly evolving to provide users with the most relevant and valuable information. By regularly producing content that addresses the needs and interests of your target audience, you can establish your website as a reliable source of information and improve your search engine rankings.

Incorporating on-page optimization techniques is another crucial element in optimizing content for search engines. This includes optimizing meta tags, headers, URLs, and image alt tags to provide search engines with relevant information about your content. Additionally, utilizing internal and external links can help search engines understand the structure of your website and improve your overall ranking.

Lastly, monitoring and analyzing your website's performance is essential in optimizing content for search engines. By utilizing various analytics tools, you can gain insights into your website's traffic, bounce rate, conversion rates, and more. This data can help you identify areas for improvement and refine your SEO strategies.

In conclusion, optimizing content for search engines is crucial for any marketer looking to maximize their marketing effects. By understanding the importance of keywords, user experience, high-quality content, on-page optimization, and performance analysis, you can significantly improve your website's visibility and attract more organic traffic. By implementing these strategies effectively, you can master search engine marketing and achieve your marketing goals.

Content Distribution and Promotion

In today's digital landscape, creating great content is just the first step. To truly maximize the impact of your marketing efforts, you need to ensure your content reaches the right audience. This is where content distribution and promotion come into play.

Content distribution refers to the various channels and platforms through which you can disseminate your content to a wider audience. It involves strategically placing your content where your target audience is most likely to discover and engage with it. By utilizing different distribution channels, you can increase your content's visibility and reach a larger number of potential customers.

One of the most effective distribution channels is search engine marketing (SEM). By optimizing your content for search engines, you can ensure that it appears prominently in search engine results pages (SERPs) when users search for relevant keywords. This not only increases your brand's visibility but also drives highly targeted traffic to your website.

Social media platforms are another powerful distribution channel. With billions of users worldwide, platforms like Facebook, Instagram, Twitter, and LinkedIn offer a vast audience for your content. By sharing your content on these platforms and engaging with your audience through likes, comments, and shares, you can amplify its reach and generate more brand awareness.

Email marketing is another valuable distribution strategy. By creating an email list of interested subscribers, you can send regular newsletters and updates containing your latest content directly to their inboxes.

This ensures that your content reaches a highly engaged audience who has already expressed interest in your brand.

In addition to distribution, effective content promotion is crucial to maximize its impact. Promotion involves actively marketing your content through various channels to increase its visibility and attract more attention. This can include tactics such as influencer marketing, guest blogging, paid advertising, and content syndication.

Influencer marketing involves partnering with influential individuals in your niche to promote your content to their followers. Their endorsement can significantly boost your content's credibility and reach. Guest blogging involves writing and publishing articles on other reputable websites within your industry, allowing you to tap into their audience and gain exposure.

Paid advertising, such as pay-per-click (PPC) campaigns, allows you to target specific keywords and demographics, ensuring that your content reaches the right audience. Content syndication involves republishing your content on third-party websites, increasing its visibility and driving more traffic back to your own site.

In conclusion, content distribution and promotion are essential components of any successful marketing strategy. By strategically distributing your content across various channels and actively promoting it to reach a wider audience, you can increase brand visibility, attract more traffic, and ultimately drive conversions. Whether you leverage search engine marketing, social media platforms, email marketing, or other tactics, the key is to ensure that your content reaches the right people at the right time.

Content Marketing Analytics

In the fast-paced world of digital marketing, it's essential to stay on top of your game and constantly evaluate the effectiveness of your strategies. This is where content marketing analytics comes into play. By harnessing the power of data and analytics, you can gain valuable insights into the impact of your content marketing efforts and make informed decisions to optimize your marketing campaigns for maximum results.

Content marketing analytics is a systematic approach to measuring and analyzing the performance of your content marketing initiatives. It involves tracking, collecting, and analyzing data from various sources to understand how your content is resonating with your target audience and driving desired outcomes. From website traffic and engagement metrics to conversion rates and customer behavior, content marketing analytics provides a comprehensive view of your marketing efforts' effects.

One of the primary benefits of content marketing analytics is its ability to shed light on the effectiveness of your content in attracting and engaging your audience. By tracking metrics like page views, time spent on page, bounce rate, and social shares, you can gauge the level of interest and engagement your content generates. This information allows you to identify which types of content are resonating with your audience and which ones may need improvement.

Moreover, content marketing analytics helps you understand the impact of your content on lead generation and sales. By analyzing conversion rates, click-through rates, and other relevant metrics, you can determine which pieces of content are driving the most conversions and revenue. This knowledge enables you to optimize your content strategy to focus on producing more of the content that generates the most significant marketing effects.

Additionally, content marketing analytics can provide insights into customer behavior and preferences. By tracking metrics such as audience demographics, device usage, and referral sources, you can gain a deep understanding of your target audience. Armed with this knowledge, you can tailor your content to meet their specific needs and preferences, increasing the likelihood of converting them into loyal customers.

To effectively harness the power of content marketing analytics, it's crucial to select the right tools and technologies that align with your marketing objectives and resources. From web analytics platforms like Google Analytics to social media monitoring tools and customer relationship management (CRM) systems, there are various tools available to help you track and analyze your content marketing performance.

In conclusion, content marketing analytics is a vital component of any successful marketing strategy. By leveraging data-driven insights, you can assess the impact of your content marketing efforts and make data-backed decisions to optimize your campaigns for better results. Whether you're a marketer, business owner, or anyone interested in enhancing their content marketing effectiveness, mastering content marketing analytics is essential in achieving your marketing goals.

Chapter 7: Search Engine Marketing Analytics

Tracking and Measuring Success

Tracking and measuring success are essential elements in any marketing campaign, including search engine marketing (SEM). Without proper tracking and measurement techniques in place, it becomes challenging to gauge the effectiveness of your efforts and make data-driven decisions to optimize your marketing strategy. In this subchapter, we will explore the importance of tracking and measuring success in SEM and provide valuable insights on how to do it effectively.

The first step in tracking and measuring success is to define your objectives clearly. Are you looking to increase website traffic, generate leads, or boost sales? By identifying your goals, you can align your tracking methods accordingly. One of the most popular tools for tracking SEM success is Google Analytics, which provides in-depth data on website traffic, conversions, and user behavior. With Google Analytics, you can track the source of your traffic, identify the most effective keywords, and measure the conversion rate of your campaigns.

Another crucial aspect of measuring success in SEM is the use of key performance indicators (KPIs). KPIs allow you to evaluate the performance of your campaigns against specific metrics. Common KPIs in SEM include click-through rate (CTR), cost per click (CPC), conversion rate, and return on investment (ROI). By regularly monitoring these KPIs, you can identify areas of improvement and optimize your campaigns for better results.

Additionally, it is vital to set up conversion tracking to measure the success of your SEM efforts accurately. Conversion tracking allows you to track specific actions or events that lead to desired outcomes, such as form submissions, purchases, or downloads. By setting up conversion tracking, you can attribute conversions to specific keywords, ads, or campaigns, enabling you to allocate your budget effectively.

Apart from online tracking tools, offline tracking methods can also be valuable in assessing the overall impact of your SEM campaigns. For example, you can implement unique coupon codes or phone numbers in your ads to track offline conversions. This enables you to measure the effectiveness of your SEM efforts in driving offline sales or leads.

In conclusion, tracking and measuring success in SEM are crucial for evaluating the impact of your marketing efforts and making data-driven decisions. By setting clear objectives, utilizing tracking tools like Google Analytics, defining KPIs, and implementing conversion tracking, you can gain valuable insights into the effectiveness of your campaigns. Remember to analyze the data regularly, identify areas for improvement, and optimize your SEM strategy accordingly. With effective tracking and measurement techniques in place, you can master search engine marketing and achieve significant marketing effects.

Tools for Search Engine Marketing Analytics

In the ever-evolving world of digital marketing, search engine marketing (SEM) has become an essential strategy for businesses across all niches. Whether you are a small business owner, a marketing professional, or simply someone interested in understanding the marketing effects of search engine optimization (SEO) and pay-per-click (PPC) advertising, this subchapter titled "Tools for Search Engine Marketing Analytics" will provide you with a comprehensive guide to mastering SEM analytics.

To effectively optimize your SEM campaigns, it is crucial to track and analyze the performance of your marketing efforts. This is where search engine marketing analytics tools come into play. These tools provide valuable insights into the effectiveness of your SEO and PPC campaigns, allowing you to make data-driven decisions and improve your marketing efforts.

One of the most popular tools for SEM analytics is Google Analytics. It provides a wealth of information about website traffic, user behavior, and conversion rates. With Google Analytics, you can track the source of your website traffic, identify the keywords that drive the most conversions, and even set up custom goals to measure specific actions on your website.

Another powerful tool for SEM analytics is Google Search Console. This tool allows you to monitor your website's performance in Google search results. It provides data on the keywords that drive organic traffic to your website, the number of impressions and clicks your website receives, and even alerts you to any issues that may be affecting your website's visibility in search results.

In addition to Google's tools, there are several other SEM analytics tools available in the market. Moz, SEMrush, and Ahrefs are popular choices for tracking keyword rankings, analyzing competitor data, and monitoring backlinks. These tools provide valuable insights into your competition's strategies and help you identify opportunities for improvement.

When using SEM analytics tools, it is important to remember that data alone is not enough. It is crucial to interpret the data in the context of your marketing goals and objectives. By understanding the metrics that matter most to your business, you can leverage the insights provided by these tools to optimize your SEM campaigns and achieve better marketing effects.

In conclusion, mastering SEM analytics is essential for anyone interested in understanding the marketing effects of search engine marketing. By utilizing tools such as Google Analytics, Google Search Console, and other SEM analytics tools, you can gain valuable insights into the performance of your SEO and PPC campaigns, make data-driven decisions, and improve your marketing efforts. So, start exploring these tools and unlock the power of SEM analytics to drive your marketing success.

Understanding Metrics and KPIs

In today's digital age, marketing efforts are no longer measured solely by intuition or gut feelings. To truly master search engine marketing, it is essential to have a deep understanding of metrics and key performance indicators (KPIs). These valuable tools provide insights into the effectiveness of marketing campaigns, allowing marketers to make data-driven decisions and optimize their strategies for maximum impact.

Metrics are quantifiable data points that measure various aspects of a marketing campaign. They provide objective information about the performance and success of marketing efforts. By analyzing metrics, marketers can gain valuable insights into customer behavior, campaign reach, engagement levels, and conversion rates.

Key performance indicators, on the other hand, are specific metrics that are chosen to reflect the goals and objectives of a marketing campaign. KPIs help marketers understand whether they are on track to achieve their desired outcomes. For instance, if the goal of a campaign is to increase website traffic, a relevant KPI might be the number of unique visitors or the bounce rate.

Understanding metrics and KPIs is crucial for marketers from all backgrounds and niches, as they serve as a common language for evaluating and comparing marketing efforts. Whether you are a small business owner, a marketing professional, or simply interested in expanding your knowledge, mastering these concepts will undoubtedly enhance your marketing effects.

One of the most important metrics in search engine marketing is click-through rate (CTR). CTR measures the percentage of users who click on a specific link or advertisement. A high CTR indicates that the ad or link is compelling and relevant to users, while a low CTR may suggest that adjustments need to be made to improve its effectiveness.

Another metric that plays a significant role in search engine marketing is conversion rate. Conversion rate measures the percentage of users who take a desired action, such as making a purchase, filling out a form, or subscribing to a newsletter. By tracking conversion rates, marketers can identify which campaigns or channels are driving the most valuable actions and allocate resources accordingly.

Other essential metrics and KPIs include cost per acquisition (CPA), return on investment (ROI), customer lifetime value (CLTV), and engagement metrics such as time on page and social media shares. Each metric provides valuable insights into different aspects of a marketing campaign and can help marketers gauge their overall success.

In conclusion, understanding metrics and KPIs is crucial for anyone involved in search engine marketing. By analyzing these quantifiable data points, marketers can gain valuable insights into campaign performance, customer behavior, and ROI. Whether you are a business owner, marketing professional, or simply interested in expanding your knowledge, mastering metrics and KPIs will undoubtedly enhance your marketing effects and help you achieve your goals.

Conversion Tracking and Analysis

In today's digital world, effective marketing is all about data-driven decision-making. Without accurate tracking and analysis, it is nearly impossible to measure the success of your marketing efforts and optimize them for maximum results. This is where conversion tracking and analysis come into play.

Conversion tracking refers to the process of monitoring and measuring the actions that users take on your website or other digital platforms. These actions, known as conversions, can vary depending on your specific marketing goals. They may include making a purchase, filling out a form, signing up for a newsletter, or even just spending a certain amount of time on a page.

The importance of conversion tracking cannot be overstated. It provides valuable insights into the effectiveness of your marketing campaigns, enabling you to identify what is working and what needs improvement. By accurately tracking conversions, you can attribute them to specific marketing channels, campaigns, or even individual ads, allowing you to allocate your budget and resources more effectively.

Fortunately, there are numerous tools and technologies available that make conversion tracking relatively easy. From basic web analytics platforms like Google Analytics to more advanced solutions that offer real-time tracking and reporting, marketers have a plethora of options to choose from. The key is to select a tool that aligns with your specific needs and goals.

Once you have set up conversion tracking, the next step is analysis. This involves interpreting the data collected and drawing meaningful insights from it. By analyzing conversion data, you can gain a deeper understanding of your target audience, their behaviors, and preferences. This information can then be used to optimize your marketing strategies, improve user experience, and drive more conversions.

When analyzing conversion data, it is important to look beyond just the numbers. Consider factors such as demographic information, device usage, and referral sources to gain a comprehensive understanding of your audience. Additionally, conduct A/B tests to compare different variations of your marketing campaigns and identify the most effective strategies.

In conclusion, conversion tracking and analysis are essential components of successful search engine marketing. By accurately tracking conversions and analyzing the data, you can refine your marketing strategies, improve targeting, and ultimately drive more conversions. Remember, data-driven decision-making is the key to mastering today's competitive marketing landscape.

A/B Testing and Optimization

In the world of search engine marketing, staying ahead of the competition is essential to drive traffic, increase conversions, and maximize ROI. One of the most effective techniques to achieve this is A/B testing and optimization. This subchapter will introduce you to the concept of A/B testing and its significance in marketing efforts.

A/B testing is the process of comparing two versions of a webpage or an element within it to determine which one performs better. By creating two variations, A and B, and splitting your audience into two groups, you can measure and analyze their responses to identify the version that generates a higher conversion rate or engagement level.

Why is A/B testing important? Well, it allows marketers to make data-driven decisions rather than relying on assumptions or personal opinions. By continuously testing and optimizing various elements such as headlines, call-to-action buttons, layouts, colors, and images, you can fine-tune your marketing efforts and improve their effectiveness.

To conduct an A/B test, you need to define your objectives and hypotheses. What specific aspect do you want to improve? What do you expect to achieve by making changes? Once you have a clear goal in mind, you can start designing your test variations. It's crucial to change only one element at a time to accurately measure its impact on user behavior.

Next, you'll need to split your audience into two random groups and direct each group to one of the test variations. It's important to ensure that the sample size is statistically significant to obtain reliable results.

Tools like Google Optimize, Optimizely, or VWO can assist you in setting up and managing A/B tests with ease.

After running the test for a sufficient period, you can analyze the data and determine the winning version based on predefined success metrics. This could be an increase in click-through rates, higher conversion rates, or longer session durations. Remember to interpret the results with statistical significance in mind, as small sample sizes may lead to misleading conclusions.

A/B testing and optimization are continuous processes. Once you have implemented changes based on the test results, it's crucial to monitor their impact and iterate further to achieve even better results. By constantly refining your marketing efforts through A/B testing, you can stay ahead of the competition and drive significant improvements in your marketing effectiveness.

In conclusion, A/B testing and optimization are vital tools for marketers in today's competitive landscape. By leveraging data-driven insights, you can make informed decisions, improve user experiences, and ultimately drive better results. So, get ready to embrace A/B testing and unlock the true potential of your marketing campaigns.

Chapter 8: Local Search Engine Marketing

Local SEO Strategies for Small Businesses

In today's digital age, it is essential for small businesses to have a strong online presence in order to succeed. One of the most effective ways to achieve this is through local SEO (Search Engine Optimization) strategies. Local SEO focuses on optimizing a website's visibility in local search results, making it easier for potential customers in the same geographical area to find and engage with a business.

For small businesses, local SEO strategies can be a game-changer. By implementing these techniques, you can increase your online visibility, drive more targeted traffic to your website, and ultimately boost your sales and revenue. Here are some effective local SEO strategies that every small business should consider:

1. Optimize your website for local keywords: Conduct thorough keyword research to identify the most relevant and high-ranking keywords for your business. Incorporate these keywords naturally throughout your website's content, including in your page titles, meta descriptions, headings, and body text.

2. Create and optimize your Google My Business listing: Google My Business is a powerful tool that allows businesses to manage their online presence across Google, including Google Maps. Ensure that your listing is complete and accurate, including your business name, address, phone number, website URL, and business hours. Encourage

customers to leave reviews, as positive reviews can significantly improve your local search rankings.

3. Build local citations: Local citations are online mentions of your business's name, address, and phone number (NAP) on other websites, directories, and social media platforms. Consistency is key here, so make sure your NAP information is accurate and consistent across all platforms.

4. Encourage online reviews: Positive online reviews not only influence potential customers but also signal to search engines that your business is reputable and trustworthy. Encourage your satisfied customers to leave reviews on platforms such as Google, Yelp, and Facebook.

5. Leverage local directories and industry-specific websites: Submit your business's information to relevant local directories and industry-specific websites. This will not only improve your local SEO but also increase your chances of being discovered by potential customers in your niche.

By implementing these local SEO strategies, small businesses can effectively increase their online visibility and attract targeted customers in their local area. However, it is important to stay up-to-date with the latest trends and algorithms in the world of SEO, as search engines are constantly evolving. Stay proactive and adapt your strategies accordingly to ensure long-term success and maximum marketing effects for your small business.

Local Directory Listings and Citations

In today's digital age, it's crucial for businesses to have a strong online presence. Whether you're a small local business or a large multinational corporation, one of the key aspects of search engine marketing is ensuring that your business is listed accurately and consistently across various online directories. This subchapter will delve into the importance of local directory listings and citations, and how they can significantly impact your marketing efforts.

Local directory listings are online directories that focus on specific geographical locations. These directories allow businesses to create listings that include important information such as their name, address, phone number, website, and other relevant details. The primary purpose of these listings is to provide potential customers with accurate and up-to-date information about your business, making it easier for them to find you.

Citations, on the other hand, refer to mentions of your business's name, address, and phone number (NAP) on other websites, even if they don't link back to your website. Citations play a crucial role in search engine optimization (SEO) as search engines use them to determine the legitimacy and authority of a business. The more consistent and accurate your citations are across different platforms, the more likely search engines will trust and rank your business higher in search results.

Having accurate and consistent local directory listings and citations can have several marketing effects for your business. Firstly, it helps improve your visibility and increases the chances of potential customers finding your business online. When people search for a particular product or service in your area, having a well-optimized local directory listing can make your business appear higher in search results, giving you a competitive advantage.

Secondly, local directory listings and citations help establish credibility and trust. When customers see your business listed in reputable directories and find consistent information about your business across multiple platforms, it instills confidence in your brand. This increased trust can lead to more conversions and repeat business.

Furthermore, local directory listings and citations can also boost your website's SEO. Search engines consider the consistency and accuracy of your business information when determining search rankings. By having consistent citations, you send strong signals to search engines that your business is reliable and trustworthy, which can positively impact your organic search rankings.

In conclusion, local directory listings and citations are a vital component of search engine marketing. They not only help potential customers find your business, but they also establish credibility and improve your website's SEO. It's crucial to ensure that your business is accurately and consistently listed across various online directories and that your citations are up-to-date and consistent. By mastering local directory listings and citations, you can effectively enhance your marketing efforts and drive more targeted traffic to your business.

Managing Online Reviews and Reputation

In today's digital age, where information is readily available at our fingertips, online reviews have become an integral part of the decision-making process for consumers. Whether it's choosing a restaurant for dinner or purchasing a new product, people rely heavily on the experiences shared by others through online reviews. As such, businesses need to be proactive in managing their online reviews and reputation to ensure they are perceived positively by potential customers.

The power of online reviews should not be underestimated. Studies have shown that a majority of consumers trust online reviews as much as personal recommendations. Therefore, it is essential for businesses to actively monitor and respond to these reviews to maintain a strong online reputation.

The first step in managing online reviews is to establish a presence on popular review platforms such as Google My Business, Yelp, TripAdvisor, and industry-specific sites. By claiming your business profile on these platforms, you can respond to reviews, update information, and engage with customers directly.

Monitoring online reviews should be an ongoing task. Regularly check these platforms for new reviews and respond promptly, regardless of whether the review is positive or negative. Responding to positive reviews shows appreciation for the customer's feedback and helps build loyalty. In the case of negative reviews, responding in a professional and empathetic manner shows that you care about addressing the customer's concerns and resolving any issues they may have had.

It's important to note that not all negative reviews are bad for business. A well-handled negative review can actually have a positive impact on your reputation. By addressing the issue publicly and offering a solution, potential customers can see that you take customer satisfaction seriously and are committed to resolving any problems that may arise.

In addition to monitoring and responding to reviews, businesses should also proactively encourage satisfied customers to leave positive reviews. This can be done through email marketing campaigns, social media posts, or by including a call-to-action on your website. Positive reviews serve as social proof and can significantly influence potential customers' decision-making process.

Furthermore, businesses should regularly analyze the feedback received through online reviews to identify any recurring issues or areas for improvement. This valuable feedback can be used to enhance product or service offerings, ultimately leading to increased customer satisfaction and positive reviews.

In conclusion, managing online reviews and reputation is crucial in today's marketing landscape. By actively monitoring and responding to reviews, encouraging positive feedback, and using the insights gained from customer feedback, businesses can build and maintain a positive online reputation that will have a significant impact on their marketing efforts in the long run.

Local Advertising and Promotions

In today's hyper-connected world, effective marketing strategies are crucial for businesses of all sizes. When it comes to promoting your products or services locally, local advertising and promotions play a vital role in driving sales and building brand awareness. This subchapter aims to provide a comprehensive guide to mastering local advertising and promotions, ensuring that your marketing efforts have a significant impact.

Local advertising refers to the promotional activities conducted within a specific geographic area to target potential customers in that region. It allows businesses to penetrate their local markets and connect with their target audience on a more personal level. From traditional methods like newspaper ads, flyers, and billboards to modern digital techniques such as search engine marketing and social media advertising, there are various avenues to explore.

One of the most effective ways to advertise locally is through search engine marketing (SEM). By utilizing search engine optimization (SEO) techniques and pay-per-click (PPC) advertising, businesses can increase their online visibility and attract local customers actively searching for their products or services. This approach ensures that your marketing efforts are not wasted on irrelevant audiences, maximizing your return on investment.

Furthermore, social media platforms offer a powerful tool for local advertising and promotions. With the ability to target specific demographics and locations, businesses can create targeted ads and engage with potential customers in their local area. Building a strong social media presence through consistent and engaging content can also significantly enhance brand awareness and customer loyalty.

In addition to online strategies, businesses should not overlook the importance of offline promotions. Local events, community sponsorships, and partnerships with other local businesses can help create a positive brand image and foster a sense of trust among the local population. By participating in local events and supporting community causes, businesses can show their commitment to the community and generate positive word-of-mouth referrals.

To ensure the effectiveness of local advertising and promotions, it is essential to measure and analyze the results of your marketing efforts. By tracking key performance indicators such as website traffic, conversions, and customer feedback, businesses can identify what works and what needs improvement. This data-driven approach allows for continuous optimization and refinement, ensuring that your local marketing strategies yield the desired outcomes.

In conclusion, local advertising and promotions are integral components of a successful marketing strategy. Whether through search engine marketing, social media advertising, or offline promotions, businesses can effectively target their local audience and drive sales. By continually analyzing and refining their marketing efforts, businesses can maximize the impact of their local advertising and promotions, ultimately achieving their marketing objectives.

Location-Based Targeting

In today's digital age, location-based targeting has emerged as a powerful tool in the world of marketing. It allows businesses to reach their target audience with precision and relevance, enhancing the overall effectiveness of their marketing efforts. Whether you are a small business owner or a marketing professional, understanding the concept of location-based targeting is crucial for success in the competitive landscape of search engine marketing.

Location-based targeting refers to the practice of tailoring marketing messages and advertisements to specific geographic locations. With the advancement of technology and the widespread use of smartphones, businesses now have access to a wealth of data on their customers' locations. This valuable information enables marketers to deliver targeted ads to individuals in a particular region, city, or even neighborhood, increasing the likelihood of conversion and customer engagement.

One of the key benefits of location-based targeting is its ability to enhance the relevance of marketing campaigns. By customizing advertisements based on the location of the consumer, businesses can ensure that their messages resonate with the target audience. For example, a restaurant in New York City can use location-based targeting to display ads to people searching for nearby dining options. This not only increases the chances of attracting customers but also saves marketing budgets by eliminating irrelevant impressions.

Location-based targeting can also help businesses analyze the impact of their marketing efforts on specific geographic regions. By tracking the performance of campaigns in different locations, marketers can gain insights into which regions are most responsive to their messages. This information can then be used to optimize future campaigns, allocate resources effectively, and maximize return on investment.

Moreover, location-based targeting allows businesses to tap into the growing trend of local search. As more and more people rely on search engines to find products and services in their vicinity, businesses can leverage this behavior to capture the attention of potential customers. By appearing in search results when someone is actively looking for a specific service in their location, businesses can significantly increase their chances of conversion.

In conclusion, location-based targeting is a game-changer in the field of search engine marketing. By harnessing the power of geographic data, businesses can deliver highly relevant advertisements and messages to their target audience. Whether you are a small business owner seeking to attract local customers or a marketing professional looking to optimize campaigns, understanding and implementing location-based targeting is essential for achieving marketing success in today's digital landscape.

Chapter 9: Mobile Search Engine Marketing

Mobile SEO Optimization Techniques

In today's digital age, it is essential for businesses to optimize their websites for mobile devices to stay ahead in the competitive online landscape. With the majority of internet users accessing the web through mobile devices, mobile SEO optimization techniques have become a crucial aspect of successful marketing strategies. This subchapter aims to provide a comprehensive guide to mastering mobile SEO optimization techniques, ensuring that your website performs effectively on various mobile devices.

1. Responsive Web Design: One of the primary techniques for mobile SEO optimization is implementing a responsive web design. This approach allows your website to adapt and display perfectly across different screen sizes and resolutions, providing a seamless user experience.

2. Mobile-Friendly Content: Creating mobile-friendly content is vital to enhance your website's mobile SEO. This includes using shorter paragraphs, concise headings, and bullet points to make your content easily readable on smaller screens.

3. Page Speed Optimization: Mobile users expect fast-loading websites, so optimizing your page speed is crucial. Compressing images, minifying CSS and JavaScript files, and leveraging browser caching are some effective techniques to improve your website's loading time.

4. Mobile Keyword Research: Conducting mobile-specific keyword research is essential to identify the search terms mobile users are likely

to use. Mobile searches often have different intent and phrasing compared to desktop searches, so adapting your keyword strategy accordingly will boost your mobile SEO efforts.

5. Voice Search Optimization: With the rise of voice assistants and smart speakers, optimizing your website for voice search is crucial for mobile SEO. Focus on long-tail conversational keywords and create content that answers common voice search queries.

6. Local SEO Optimization: For businesses targeting local customers, optimizing your website for local search is crucial. Ensure your business information is accurate and consistent across online directories and use location-specific keywords to improve your mobile SEO.

7. User Experience Optimization: Mobile users value a seamless and intuitive user experience. Optimize your website's navigation, minimize pop-ups, improve readability, and ensure that buttons and links are easily clickable on mobile screens.

By implementing these mobile SEO optimization techniques, you can improve your website's visibility, attract more mobile users, and stay ahead of the competition. Keep in mind that mobile SEO is an ongoing process, and staying up-to-date with the latest trends and algorithm changes is crucial to maintain your website's mobile performance.

Mobile Advertising Strategies

In today's digital age, where smartphones have become an integral part of our lives, mobile advertising has emerged as a powerful tool for marketers to reach their target audience. With millions of people using their mobile devices to browse the internet, shop online, and interact on social media, it is essential for marketers to develop effective mobile advertising strategies to maximize their marketing efforts.

One of the key strategies in mobile advertising is to optimize your website and landing pages for mobile devices. With the majority of internet users accessing websites through their smartphones, it is crucial to ensure that your website is mobile-friendly. This includes having a responsive design that adapts to different screen sizes, optimizing loading times, and providing a seamless user experience. By providing a user-friendly mobile experience, you can increase engagement and conversions.

Another effective strategy in mobile advertising is to utilize location-based targeting. With the GPS capabilities of mobile devices, marketers can target users based on their location and deliver personalized ads. For example, a restaurant can target users who are in close proximity and offer them a special discount or promotion. By leveraging location-based targeting, marketers can reach their audience at the right place and time, increasing the chances of conversion.

Furthermore, mobile advertising offers the opportunity to leverage various ad formats to engage users. From banner ads to video ads and interactive ads, there are numerous options to capture the attention of mobile users. However, it is crucial to create compelling and visually appealing ads that resonate with the target audience. Additionally, marketers should consider the context in which the ads are displayed to ensure relevancy and maximize impact.

Moreover, mobile advertising also provides the opportunity to leverage social media platforms. With the majority of social media users accessing these platforms through their mobile devices, marketers can use social media advertising to target and engage their audience effectively. By utilizing features such as sponsored posts, stories, and influencer collaborations, marketers can increase brand awareness and drive conversions.

In conclusion, mobile advertising strategies are essential for marketers to effectively reach their target audience in today's mobile-driven world. By optimizing websites for mobile devices, utilizing location-based targeting, leveraging various ad formats, and utilizing social media platforms, marketers can maximize the impact of their marketing efforts and drive desired marketing effects. By staying up-to-date with the latest trends and continuously optimizing mobile advertising strategies, marketers can stay ahead of the competition and achieve success in their digital marketing campaigns.

Responsive Web Design for Mobile

In today's digital age, where smartphones and tablets have become an integral part of our lives, it is of utmost importance for businesses to optimize their websites for mobile devices. This subchapter on Responsive Web Design for Mobile aims to provide a comprehensive guide for everyone, with a particular focus on its marketing effects.

Responsive web design refers to the approach of creating websites that adapt and respond to different screen sizes and devices. With the ever-increasing usage of mobile devices to access the internet, having a responsive website is no longer an option but a necessity. This subchapter will delve into the various aspects of responsive web design and its impact on marketing efforts.

Firstly, we will explore the importance of mobile-friendly websites in the modern marketing landscape. With more and more users accessing websites through their smartphones, businesses need to ensure that their websites provide a seamless and optimized experience across all devices. A responsive website not only enhances user experience but also boosts search engine rankings, resulting in increased organic traffic and improved conversion rates.

Next, we will discuss the key elements of responsive web design. From fluid grids and flexible images to media queries and mobile-first design principles, we will explore the essential components that make a website responsive. By understanding these elements, marketers can collaborate effectively with web developers to create a visually appealing and user-friendly mobile experience.

Furthermore, this subchapter will delve into the benefits of responsive web design for marketing efforts. A responsive website ensures consistent branding and messaging across all devices, allowing businesses to maintain a cohesive and professional image. It also enables marketers to track and analyze user behavior accurately, optimizing their campaigns based on data-driven insights.

Lastly, we will explore best practices and emerging trends in responsive web design. From the importance of fast-loading pages to the integration of mobile-specific features, we will discuss strategies that marketers can employ to stay ahead of the competition and deliver exceptional mobile experiences.

In conclusion, responsive web design for mobile is an essential aspect of modern marketing. This subchapter aims to equip everyone with the knowledge and tools necessary to create mobile-friendly websites that enhance marketing efforts. By embracing responsive web design, businesses can effectively engage with their target audience, improve brand perception, and drive measurable results in today's mobile-centric world.

Mobile App Marketing

In today's digital age, mobile apps have become an integral part of our lives. From ordering food to managing finances, there seems to be an app for everything. However, with millions of apps available in various app stores, how can app developers ensure that their app stands out from the crowd and reaches their target audience? This is where mobile app marketing comes into play.

Mobile app marketing is a strategic approach to promote and advertise mobile applications to increase their visibility, downloads, and user engagement. It involves a combination of techniques and strategies tailored to the unique challenges and opportunities presented by the mobile app ecosystem. This subchapter aims to provide a comprehensive guide to mastering mobile app marketing for everyone, regardless of their level of expertise in marketing.

First and foremost, understanding the target audience is crucial. By identifying the target audience's needs, preferences, and behaviors, marketers can create effective marketing strategies that resonate with potential app users. This includes conducting market research, analyzing user demographics, and studying competitors' tactics.

One of the key aspects of mobile app marketing is App Store Optimization (ASO). ASO involves optimizing the app's metadata, including the app title, description, keywords, and screenshots, to improve its visibility in app store search results. This subchapter will delve into the best practices of ASO, including keyword research, A/B testing, and monitoring user reviews.

Additionally, the subchapter will cover various channels and techniques for promoting mobile apps. These include social media marketing, influencer partnerships, content marketing, and paid advertising. Each channel brings its own unique benefits and challenges, and marketers need to carefully select the right mix based on their target audience and budget.

Furthermore, user engagement and retention are vital for the long-term success of a mobile app. The subchapter will explore strategies for increasing user engagement through push notifications, in-app messaging, personalized experiences, and gamification. It will also address techniques for measuring and analyzing app performance, such as user analytics and conversion tracking.

For those new to mobile app marketing, this subchapter will serve as a comprehensive guide to understanding the fundamentals and implementing effective strategies. For experienced marketers, it will provide valuable insights and advanced techniques to optimize their mobile app marketing efforts.

Mastering mobile app marketing is essential for app developers and marketers aiming to maximize the reach and impact of their mobile applications. It is a constantly evolving field, and staying updated with the latest trends and best practices is crucial for success. This subchapter aims to equip readers with the knowledge and tools necessary to excel in the ever-changing landscape of mobile app marketing.

Voice Search Optimization

As technology continues to advance, voice search has emerged as a popular and convenient way for users to interact with search engines. With the rapid growth of virtual assistants like Siri, Google Assistant, and Amazon Alexa, voice search has become an integral part of our daily lives. This subchapter on Voice Search Optimization aims to provide a comprehensive guide for everyone, especially those interested in the marketing effects of this emerging trend.

Voice search optimization refers to the process of optimizing your website or content to enhance its visibility and relevance in voice search results. Traditional search engine optimization (SEO) techniques are still essential, but voice search introduces new factors that need to be considered. This subchapter will delve into these factors and provide practical strategies for optimizing your website for voice search.

One crucial aspect of voice search optimization is understanding how people use voice search. Voice queries tend to be longer and more conversational compared to typed queries. Users often ask complete questions, seeking immediate answers or assistance. Therefore, it is crucial to optimize your content to match these conversational queries. This subchapter will guide you through the process of identifying and incorporating the right long-tail keywords to enhance your website's visibility in voice search results.

Another critical factor in voice search optimization is ensuring your website is mobile-friendly and loads quickly. Voice search is predominantly used on mobile devices, and search engines prioritize websites that provide a seamless mobile experience. This subchapter will discuss the importance of mobile optimization and provide tips for improving your website's performance.

Additionally, this subchapter will explore the impact of local search on voice search results. With virtual assistants often providing local business recommendations, it is vital for businesses to optimize their online presence for local search. Strategies such as creating and optimizing Google My Business listings and managing online reviews will be discussed in detail.

By mastering voice search optimization, you can significantly improve your website's visibility and attract a wider audience. Whether you are a business owner, marketer, or simply interested in the marketing effects of voice search, this subchapter will equip you with the knowledge and tools needed to stay ahead in the ever-evolving world of search engine marketing.

Chapter 10: Advanced Search Engine Marketing Strategies

Remarketing and Retargeting

Remarketing and retargeting are two powerful strategies within the realm of search engine marketing that can greatly enhance marketing efforts and generate significant results. In this subchapter, we will delve into the concepts of remarketing and retargeting and explore how they can be effectively utilized to maximize marketing effects.

Remarketing refers to the practice of targeting individuals who have previously interacted with a brand or visited a website. It involves displaying relevant ads to these users as they browse the internet, encouraging them to return and complete a desired action. By leveraging data collected from website visitors, remarketing allows marketers to create highly personalized and targeted campaigns.

Retargeting, on the other hand, focuses on reconnecting with users who have shown interest in a particular product or service. It involves displaying ads to these individuals across various platforms and websites they visit, with the aim of keeping the brand or product top-of-mind and ultimately driving conversions. Retargeting can be particularly effective in reaching potential customers who may have abandoned their shopping carts or failed to complete a desired action.

Both remarketing and retargeting offer numerous benefits for marketers. By targeting individuals who have already engaged with a brand or expressed interest in a product, these strategies enable marketers to deliver highly relevant and personalized ads, increasing the likelihood of conversion. Additionally, remarketing and retargeting campaigns can significantly improve brand recall and visibility, reinforcing the brand message and enhancing overall marketing effects.

To implement effective remarketing and retargeting campaigns, marketers should carefully segment their audience and tailor their messaging accordingly. By understanding the specific needs and preferences of different customer segments, marketers can create compelling ads that speak directly to each group. It is also crucial to closely monitor campaign performance and optimize accordingly, ensuring that ads are being displayed at the right time and in the right places to maximize impact.

In conclusion, remarketing and retargeting are powerful tools that can greatly enhance marketing effects. By targeting individuals who have already engaged with a brand or expressed interest in a product, marketers can deliver highly personalized and relevant ads, increasing the likelihood of conversion. By carefully segmenting the audience, tailoring messaging, and monitoring campaign performance, marketers can maximize the impact of remarketing and retargeting campaigns and achieve significant results.

Video Advertising on Search Engines

In today's digital age, video advertising has emerged as a powerful tool for marketers to engage with their target audience. With the rise of online video consumption, search engines have become an essential platform to promote and distribute video content. This subchapter explores the world of video advertising on search engines and its impact on marketing efforts.

Search engines, such as Google and Bing, are not only used for finding information but also serve as a gateway for discovering engaging video content. By incorporating video advertising into search engine marketing strategies, marketers can leverage the vast reach and targeting capabilities of these platforms to connect with their desired audience.

One of the key advantages of video advertising on search engines is the ability to reach a highly targeted audience. Marketers can specify their target audience based on demographics, interests, and search behavior, ensuring that their video ads are shown to the right people at the right time. This level of precision targeting allows for a more efficient use of marketing budgets and increases the likelihood of conversions.

Additionally, video advertising on search engines provides a unique opportunity to engage users with captivating visual content. Unlike traditional text-based ads, video ads have the power to convey emotions, tell stories, and showcase products or services in a more compelling manner. This immersive experience not only helps in capturing the attention of viewers but also enhances brand recall and recognition.

Another significant advantage of video advertising on search engines is the ability to measure and analyze campaign performance. Marketers can track various metrics, such as views, click-through rates, and conversions, to evaluate the effectiveness of their video ads. This data-driven approach allows for continuous optimization and refinement of video campaigns to achieve the desired marketing objectives.

Despite its numerous benefits, video advertising on search engines does require careful planning and execution. Marketers need to create engaging and relevant video content that aligns with their overall marketing strategy. It is important to consider factors such as video length, call-to-action, and optimizing for mobile devices to maximize the impact of video ads.

In conclusion, video advertising on search engines presents a vast opportunity for marketers to enhance their marketing efforts. By leveraging the wide reach, targeting capabilities, and engaging nature of video ads, marketers can connect with their target audience in a more meaningful way. However, it is crucial to develop a well-thought-out video advertising strategy and continuously analyze and optimize campaigns to achieve the desired marketing effects.

International Search Engine Marketing

In today's interconnected world, the internet has become the backbone of global communication and commerce. As businesses strive to reach a wider audience and expand their market reach, search engine marketing (SEM) has emerged as a vital tool in their marketing arsenal. One of the key aspects of SEM is International Search Engine Marketing, which focuses on reaching and engaging with audiences in different countries and regions across the globe.

International Search Engine Marketing involves tailoring marketing strategies to specific countries or regions, taking into account cultural nuances, language preferences, and search engine algorithms. It enables businesses to tap into new markets, increase brand visibility, and drive targeted traffic to their websites. By optimizing their online presence, businesses can attract potential customers from around the world, thereby maximizing their marketing effects.

When it comes to International Search Engine Marketing, it is crucial to understand the various components involved. Firstly, keyword research plays a vital role in identifying the search terms and phrases that are popular among the target audience in different countries. By incorporating these keywords into their website content, businesses can improve their rankings on international search engine result pages (SERPs).

Furthermore, localization is another key aspect of International Search Engine Marketing. This involves adapting the content, language, and design of a website to suit the preferences and expectations of a specific country or region. By tailoring their website to the local culture, businesses can establish trust, resonate with the target audience, and enhance their marketing effects.

Another important consideration in International Search Engine Marketing is the selection of search engines. While Google may be the dominant search engine in many countries, there are several regions where local search engines have a significant market share. By targeting these search engines, businesses can gain a competitive edge and maximize their visibility in specific markets.

Additionally, International Search Engine Marketing also encompasses paid search advertising through platforms like Google Ads and Bing Ads. By creating targeted campaigns and utilizing geo-targeting options, businesses can display their ads to relevant audiences in different countries, further enhancing their marketing efforts.

In conclusion, International Search Engine Marketing is a crucial aspect of modern marketing strategies. By optimizing their online presence, tailoring their content to specific regions, and utilizing targeted advertising, businesses can expand their reach globally and maximize their marketing effects. With the ever-increasing connectivity of the internet, International Search Engine Marketing is a powerful tool for businesses of all sizes and niches to succeed in the global marketplace.

Influencer Marketing in Search Engine Marketing

In today's digital age, businesses have recognized the power of search engine marketing (SEM) in reaching their target audience and driving online visibility. However, as the online landscape becomes increasingly saturated, marketers are constantly seeking innovative ways to stand out from the crowd and capture the attention of potential customers. One such method that has gained significant popularity is influencer marketing.

Influencer marketing combines the strengths of SEM and the power of social media influencers to create effective and impactful marketing campaigns. By leveraging the authority and reach of influential individuals in specific niches, businesses can amplify their brand message and establish credibility among their target audience.

When it comes to SEM, influencers play a crucial role in enhancing marketing efforts. By partnering with influencers who align with their brand values and target audience, businesses can tap into their existing fan base and benefit from their expertise, trust, and loyal following. Influencers can create authentic and engaging content that resonates with their audience, which can significantly increase brand visibility and drive traffic to a company's website or landing page.

Moreover, influencers can also optimize search engine results by incorporating relevant keywords and engaging content in their posts. This not only improves a brand's visibility in search engine rankings but also increases the chances of generating organic traffic. Additionally, influencers can provide valuable backlinks to a company's website, which further boosts its search engine optimization (SEO) efforts.

Influencer marketing in SEM also offers the advantage of precise targeting. With the help of influencers, businesses can directly reach their niche audience, ensuring that their marketing efforts are directed towards individuals who are most likely to convert into customers. This targeted approach eliminates wastage of resources and maximizes the return on investment (ROI) of marketing campaigns.

To successfully incorporate influencer marketing into SEM, it is crucial for businesses to identify and collaborate with the right influencers. Thorough research should be conducted to ensure that the influencers' values, audience demographics, and engagement levels align with the brand's objectives. Additionally, clear communication and mutual understanding between the brand and the influencers are key to executing effective campaigns.

In conclusion, influencer marketing in search engine marketing offers a powerful way for businesses to enhance their online visibility, drive targeted traffic, and establish credibility among their target audience. By leveraging the authority and reach of influencers, brands can create impactful and engaging marketing campaigns that yield significant results. However, it is important for businesses to carefully select and collaborate with the right influencers to ensure the success of their campaigns.

Artificial Intelligence and Machine Learning in SEM

In recent years, the field of search engine marketing (SEM) has undergone a revolutionary transformation with the integration of artificial intelligence (AI) and machine learning (ML) technologies. These advancements have significantly enhanced marketing strategies and their effects on various niches. Today, AI and ML are indispensable tools for marketers of all levels, enabling them to optimize their SEM campaigns and achieve remarkable results.

One of the most significant benefits of AI and ML in SEM is their ability to analyze vast amounts of data quickly and accurately. These technologies can process complex algorithms and patterns, allowing marketers to gain valuable insights into consumer behavior, preferences, and search patterns. By understanding these intricate details, marketers can create tailored and personalized advertising campaigns that resonate with their target audience.

Furthermore, AI and ML play a vital role in improving ad targeting and optimization. With the help of these technologies, marketers can identify the most relevant keywords, phrases, and demographics for their ads. AI-powered algorithms can analyze user data, search history, and browsing behavior to determine the best ad placements, timing, and targeting options. This level of precision ensures that ads are shown to the right people at the right time, maximizing the chances of conversions and boosting marketing effects.

Another area where AI and ML are transforming SEM is in ad copy creation. These technologies can generate compelling and persuasive ad copy by analyzing historical data and understanding language patterns. Marketers can effortlessly create impactful ads that resonate with their target audience, resulting in higher click-through rates and engagement.

Moreover, AI and ML aid in monitoring and optimizing SEM campaigns in real-time. These technologies can continuously analyze campaign performance, detect trends, and make intelligent adjustments to improve results. Marketers can leverage AI-powered tools to automate bid management, budget allocation, and ad scheduling, saving time and resources while maximizing marketing effects.

In conclusion, the integration of AI and ML in SEM has revolutionized the marketing landscape, providing marketers with powerful tools to enhance their strategies and boost marketing effects. By leveraging these technologies, marketers can gain valuable insights into consumer behavior, optimize ad targeting, create persuasive ad copy, and monitor campaign performance in real-time. Whether you are a seasoned marketer or a newcomer to the field, understanding and harnessing the power of AI and ML in SEM is essential to succeed in today's competitive digital landscape.

Chapter 11: Search Engine Marketing for E-commerce

E-commerce SEO Strategies

In today's digital age, having a strong online presence is crucial for businesses of all sizes. For e-commerce websites, search engine optimization (SEO) plays a vital role in driving organic traffic and increasing sales. In this subchapter, we will delve deep into effective e-commerce SEO strategies that can help your business thrive in the competitive online marketplace.

1. Keyword Research: The foundation of any successful SEO strategy is thorough keyword research. Identify the keywords and phrases that your target audience is using to search for products or services similar to yours. Utilize keyword research tools to discover high-volume, low-competition keywords that can be integrated into your website's content, meta tags, and product descriptions.

2. On-Page Optimization: Optimize your e-commerce website's on-page elements to improve its visibility in search engine results pages (SERPs). This includes optimizing meta titles, meta descriptions, URLs, and header tags. Ensure that each page has unique, descriptive content that is relevant to the keywords you are targeting.

3. High-Quality Product Descriptions: Craft compelling and unique product descriptions that not only appeal to your customers but also include relevant keywords. Avoid duplicating manufacturer-provided descriptions, as this can hinder your website's search rankings. Focus

on providing detailed information, highlighting product features, benefits, and any unique selling points.

4. User Experience: User experience (UX) plays a vital role in SEO. A well-designed and user-friendly e-commerce website not only enhances customer satisfaction but also improves search engine rankings. Ensure your website is mobile-friendly, loads quickly, and has intuitive navigation. Implement features such as faceted search, product reviews, and personalized recommendations to enhance the overall user experience.

5. Link Building: Building high-quality backlinks is essential for improving your website's authority and search rankings. Reach out to influential bloggers, industry experts, and relevant websites to secure backlinks. Additionally, leverage social media platforms to share your content and encourage others to link back to your e-commerce website.

6. Technical SEO: Pay attention to technical SEO aspects, such as website speed, crawlability, and indexability. Optimize your website's code, use XML sitemaps, and fix any broken links or errors. Regularly monitor and analyze your website's performance using tools like Google Analytics to identify and address any technical issues that may hinder your SEO efforts.

By implementing these e-commerce SEO strategies, you can improve your website's visibility, attract targeted traffic, and increase conversions. Remember to continually monitor and adapt your strategies based on search engine algorithm updates and changes in consumer behavior. With a comprehensive and well-executed SEO plan, your e-commerce business can thrive in the digital landscape.

Product Listing Ads (PLA)

In today's digital age, it is imperative for businesses to stay ahead of the game when it comes to marketing their products. One effective strategy that has gained significant traction in recent years is the use of Product Listing Ads (PLA). This subchapter aims to provide a comprehensive understanding of PLA and its impact on marketing efforts.

Product Listing Ads, also known as PLA, are a type of online advertising that allows businesses to promote their products directly on search engine result pages. Unlike traditional text-based ads, PLAs are visually appealing and provide users with detailed product information such as images, prices, and even customer reviews. This makes it easier for potential customers to make informed purchasing decisions.

One of the key advantages of using PLAs is their ability to target specific audiences. With the help of advanced targeting options, businesses can display their ads to users who are actively searching for products similar to theirs. This ensures that the right people are seeing their ads, increasing the chances of conversion and return on investment.

Furthermore, PLAs have a higher click-through rate compared to text-based ads. The visual nature of these ads captures users' attention and entices them to click for more information. This increased engagement can lead to higher website traffic and ultimately more sales.

Another benefit of PLAs is the ability to easily measure their effectiveness. With the help of analytics tools, businesses can track the performance of their ads, including impressions, clicks, and conversions. This data provides valuable insights into customer behavior and allows businesses to optimize their campaigns for better results.

PLAs are particularly effective for e-commerce businesses as they provide a direct link to the product page. This eliminates the need for users to navigate through multiple pages, making the purchasing process quicker and more convenient. Moreover, the visual nature of PLAs allows businesses to showcase their products in a visually appealing manner, increasing the likelihood of purchase.

In conclusion, Product Listing Ads (PLA) are a powerful tool in the world of search engine marketing. Their visual appeal, targeted approach, and measurable results make them a valuable asset for businesses across various niches. Whether you are an e-commerce business or a small local retailer, integrating PLAs into your marketing strategy can significantly enhance your marketing efforts and drive tangible results.

Shopping Campaigns

Shopping campaigns are an essential component of search engine marketing, particularly for businesses looking to expand their online presence and drive sales. In this subchapter, we will delve into the intricacies of shopping campaigns, discussing their significance, benefits, and strategies for maximizing their marketing effects.

Shopping campaigns, also known as product listing ads (PLAs), are a type of online advertising that showcases products directly within search engine results. These campaigns display relevant product information, including images, prices, and merchant names, enticing potential customers to click on the ads and make a purchase. Unlike traditional text-based advertisements, shopping campaigns allow businesses to visually showcase their products, making them more appealing and increasing the likelihood of conversions.

One of the key benefits of shopping campaigns is their ability to reach a highly targeted audience. By utilizing product attributes such as category, brand, and price, businesses can ensure their ads are displayed to users actively searching for specific products. This targeted approach not only increases the chances of converting leads into customers but also improves the overall return on investment (ROI) of the campaign.

To maximize the marketing effects of shopping campaigns, businesses need to develop a comprehensive strategy. Firstly, it is crucial to optimize product feeds, which act as the foundation for these campaigns. Product feeds should contain accurate and detailed information about products, including titles, descriptions, and images.

By properly optimizing product feeds, businesses can improve the visibility and relevance of their ads, leading to higher click-through rates and conversions.

Additionally, businesses should carefully structure their shopping campaigns to align with their marketing goals. Creating separate campaigns for different product categories, brands, or price ranges allows for better control over budget allocation and bidding strategies. This segmentation enables businesses to optimize campaigns based on the performance of specific products, ensuring maximum ROI.

Furthermore, regularly monitoring and analyzing campaign performance is vital for ongoing success. Utilizing analytics tools provided by search engines, businesses can gain valuable insights into key metrics such as click-through rates, conversion rates, and cost per click. These metrics help identify areas for improvement and enable businesses to make data-driven decisions to optimize their shopping campaigns.

In conclusion, shopping campaigns play a crucial role in search engine marketing, offering businesses the opportunity to showcase their products directly within search results. By implementing effective strategies such as optimizing product feeds, structuring campaigns, and analyzing performance, businesses can maximize the marketing effects of shopping campaigns and drive substantial growth in online sales. Whether you are a small business owner, a marketing professional, or an aspiring entrepreneur, understanding and harnessing the power of shopping campaigns is essential for achieving success in today's digital landscape.

Dynamic Remarketing for E-commerce

In the fast-paced world of online marketing, staying ahead of the competition is crucial. One effective strategy that has gained significant traction in recent years is dynamic remarketing for e-commerce. This subchapter will delve into the power of dynamic remarketing and its potential to revolutionize your marketing efforts.

Dynamic remarketing is a technique that allows e-commerce businesses to personalize their advertising campaigns based on users' browsing behavior and purchase history. By leveraging the vast amount of data collected from users' interactions with your website, you can create highly targeted and relevant ads that are more likely to engage and convert potential customers.

The key to successful dynamic remarketing lies in its ability to deliver tailored messages to specific individuals. By dynamically displaying products or services that users have previously shown interest in, you can create a sense of familiarity and increase the likelihood of conversion. For example, if a user has recently browsed a specific product on your website, dynamic remarketing can show them an ad highlighting that very same product, thus reminding them of their initial interest and prompting them to make a purchase.

Furthermore, dynamic remarketing enables you to optimize your advertising budget by focusing on users who are more likely to convert. By analyzing users' behavior, such as the time spent on specific pages or the number of items added to their cart, you can prioritize your ad spend on those individuals who have demonstrated higher intent to purchase. This way, you can maximize your return on investment and ensure that your marketing efforts are directed towards the most promising leads.

Implementing dynamic remarketing requires a solid understanding of data analysis and ad customization techniques. However, with the right tools and strategies in place, this powerful marketing approach can significantly enhance your e-commerce business's growth and revenue. Whether you are a seasoned marketer or a beginner in the field, mastering dynamic remarketing is essential for optimizing your marketing effects and staying competitive in the ever-evolving online marketplace.

In conclusion, dynamic remarketing for e-commerce is a game-changer in the world of online marketing. By tailoring your ads to individual users based on their browsing behavior and purchase history, you can create personalized and compelling messages that increase the likelihood of conversions. This subchapter has explored the potential of dynamic remarketing and highlighted its ability to optimize your advertising budget and maximize your return on investment. Whether you are a marketing professional or someone interested in the field, understanding and implementing dynamic remarketing is crucial for staying ahead in today's competitive e-commerce landscape.

Conversion Rate Optimization for E-commerce

In today's digital age, optimizing conversion rates is essential for the success of any e-commerce business. Whether you are just starting out or have an established online store, mastering the art of Conversion Rate Optimization (CRO) can significantly impact your marketing efforts and ultimately lead to higher sales.

CRO is the process of enhancing your website or landing page to convert more visitors into customers. It involves analyzing user behavior, making data-driven decisions, and implementing various strategies to improve the overall user experience and increase conversion rates.

One of the key elements of CRO is understanding your target audience. By conducting thorough market research and analyzing customer demographics, preferences, and buying patterns, you can tailor your website to meet their specific needs. This includes optimizing your site's layout, navigation, and content to ensure a seamless and user-friendly experience.

Another crucial aspect of CRO is effective call-to-action (CTA) placement. A well-placed CTA can significantly influence a visitor's decision-making process. By experimenting with different CTA designs, colors, and placements, you can determine which ones generate the highest conversion rates. Additionally, implementing persuasive and compelling copy that highlights the benefits of your products or services can further entice visitors to take action.

Furthermore, optimizing your website for mobile devices is essential in today's mobile-first era. With the majority of online traffic coming from smartphones and tablets, it is crucial to ensure that your e-commerce site is mobile-responsive and offers a seamless browsing and purchasing experience. A slow or unresponsive mobile site can lead to high bounce rates and missed sales opportunities.

Utilizing A/B testing is another valuable technique in CRO. By creating different variations of your website or landing page and testing them against each other, you can identify which elements or design choices have a significant impact on conversion rates. This data-driven approach allows you to make informed decisions and continuously improve your site's performance.

In conclusion, Conversion Rate Optimization is a vital component of any e-commerce marketing strategy. By understanding your target audience, optimizing your website's layout and content, strategically placing CTAs, optimizing for mobile, and utilizing A/B testing, you can maximize your conversion rates and ultimately drive more sales. Remember, CRO is an ongoing process that requires constant analysis, experimentation, and adaptation to the ever-evolving digital landscape.

Chapter 12: Future Trends in Search Engine Marketing

Voice Search and Virtual Assistants

In today's fast-paced digital era, technology continues to evolve and reshape the way we interact with the world around us. One of the most significant advancements in recent years is the rise of voice search and virtual assistants. This subchapter will delve into the world of voice search and virtual assistants and their profound effects on marketing.

Voice search refers to the act of using spoken words to conduct an online search. With the advent of smart speakers and mobile devices, voice search has become increasingly popular. Virtual assistants, such as Amazon's Alexa, Apple's Siri, Google Assistant, and Microsoft's Cortana, are the driving forces behind this transformation. These virtual assistants interpret voice commands and provide users with information, assistance, and perform various tasks.

The impact of voice search and virtual assistants on marketing is undeniable. As more and more users rely on voice commands to search for information, businesses must adapt their marketing strategies accordingly. Optimizing content for voice search has become crucial to ensure visibility and relevance in search engine results.

When it comes to voice search, long-tail keywords play a significant role. Unlike traditional text-based searches, voice queries tend to be more conversational and natural-sounding. Therefore, marketers must focus on incorporating long-tail keywords that align with users' spoken queries to increase their chances of appearing in voice search results.

Furthermore, the rise of virtual assistants has opened up new avenues for businesses to engage with their customers. Brands can now develop voice-activated applications or "skills" that allow users to interact with their products or services in innovative ways. By incorporating virtual assistants into their marketing strategy, businesses can enhance customer experiences and build stronger brand loyalty.

However, it's essential to remember that the effects of voice search and virtual assistants on marketing are still evolving. As technology continues to advance, marketers must stay up-to-date with the latest trends and adapt their strategies accordingly. Voice search optimization and virtual assistant integration are not mere options but necessary components of a successful marketing campaign.

In conclusion, voice search and virtual assistants have revolutionized the way we search for information and interact with technology. With their increasing popularity, businesses must embrace these advancements and adapt their marketing strategies to remain competitive. By optimizing content for voice search and integrating virtual assistants into their campaigns, marketers can harness the power of this technology to connect with their target audience and drive marketing effects like never before.

Mobile-First Indexing

In today's digital world, where smartphones have become an integral part of our lives, it's no surprise that businesses are increasingly focusing on mobile marketing. With the majority of internet users accessing websites through their mobile devices, it has become crucial for marketers to optimize their online presence for mobile-first indexing.

Mobile-first indexing is a concept introduced by search engines to ensure that websites are ranked based on their mobile version rather than the desktop version. This shift in prioritization is a response to the growing number of mobile users and the need to provide them with a seamless browsing experience.

For everyone involved in the world of marketing, understanding the implications of mobile-first indexing is vital. It affects not only website rankings but also user experience and conversion rates. With search engines favoring mobile-friendly websites, marketers must adapt their strategies to stay ahead of the competition.

One of the key effects of mobile-first indexing is the need for responsive web design. Websites that are not optimized for mobile devices may experience a decline in search engine rankings. Therefore, it is crucial for marketers to ensure that their websites are mobile-friendly, with responsive designs that adjust seamlessly to different screen sizes.

Additionally, page loading speed plays a significant role in mobile-first indexing. As mobile users expect instant access to information, search engines prioritize websites that load quickly on mobile devices.

Marketers need to optimize their websites by compressing images, minimizing code, and leveraging caching techniques to enhance the loading speed.

Furthermore, the content on mobile websites should be equivalent to the desktop version. Marketers must ensure that the mobile version contains all the essential information and features available on the desktop version. This includes maintaining consistent branding, providing easy navigation, and making sure that forms and calls-to-action are easily accessible on mobile devices.

By embracing mobile-first indexing, marketers can tap into the vast potential of the mobile market and enhance their marketing efforts. They can reach a wider audience, improve user experience, and ultimately drive more conversions. It is essential to stay up-to-date with the latest mobile marketing trends and strategies to ensure continued success in the ever-evolving digital landscape.

In conclusion, mobile-first indexing is a game-changer in the world of search engine marketing. Marketers must prioritize mobile optimization to improve their website rankings, enhance user experience, and increase conversions. By adopting responsive web design, optimizing page loading speed, and maintaining consistent and accessible content across devices, marketers can master mobile-first indexing and achieve their marketing goals in the mobile era.

Personalization in Search Engine Marketing

In today's digital age, search engine marketing has become an essential tool for businesses to reach their target audience effectively. However, with the ever-increasing competition in the online marketplace, it is crucial to stand out from the crowd and provide a personalized experience to your customers. This is where personalization in search engine marketing comes into play.

Personalization refers to tailoring marketing efforts to meet the individual needs and preferences of each customer. It involves using data and analytics to understand customer behavior and deliver relevant and customized content. By incorporating personalization into your search engine marketing strategy, you can enhance the effectiveness of your marketing efforts and improve customer satisfaction.

One of the key benefits of personalization in search engine marketing is the ability to deliver highly targeted ads to specific customer segments. By analyzing user data such as search history, demographics, and browsing behavior, marketers can create personalized ads that resonate with their target audience. This not only increases the chances of conversion but also enhances the overall user experience.

Furthermore, personalization allows businesses to create dynamic landing pages that adapt to each user's preferences. By displaying relevant content and offers based on individual customer data, businesses can increase engagement and drive more conversions. For example, if a customer has previously shown interest in a particular product, a personalized landing page can showcase related products or offer exclusive discounts, increasing the likelihood of a purchase.

Moreover, personalization in search engine marketing enables businesses to optimize their search engine ranking. By analyzing user search queries and preferences, businesses can tailor their content to match the needs of their target audience. This not only improves search engine visibility but also increases the chances of organic traffic and conversions.

In conclusion, personalization in search engine marketing is a powerful tool that can significantly impact marketing efforts. By analyzing customer data and delivering tailored content and ads, businesses can enhance customer satisfaction, increase conversions, and optimize search engine ranking. Embracing personalization in search engine marketing is essential for any business looking to stay competitive in today's digital landscape.

Augmented Reality and Visual Search

In today's digital age, technology has revolutionized the way we search for information, products, and services. One of the most exciting developments in this field is the integration of augmented reality (AR) and visual search into the realm of marketing. These cutting-edge technologies are transforming the way businesses connect with their target audience, enhancing user experiences, and driving marketing efforts to new heights.

Augmented reality refers to the integration of digital information or virtual objects into the real world. It allows users to interact with computer-generated images or video content in real-time, superimposed onto their physical environment. This technology has gained significant popularity in recent years, thanks to the widespread availability of smartphones and other smart devices. From virtual try-on experiences for clothing and accessories to interactive gaming applications, AR is reshaping the way consumers engage with brands.

Visual search, on the other hand, enables users to search for information using images rather than text-based queries. By analyzing the visual features of an image, such as shapes, colors, and patterns, visual search engines can identify and provide relevant results. This technology has gained momentum due to the increasing number of online shoppers and the desire for a seamless shopping experience. With visual search, users can simply snap a photo of a product they like and instantly find similar items available for purchase.

The combination of augmented reality and visual search has immense potential for marketing effects. Brands can leverage these technologies to engage with their audience in innovative ways. For instance, AR-powered advertising campaigns can allow users to virtually try on products, envision how furniture would look in their homes, or even experience a destination before booking a trip. This not only enhances user engagement but also increases the likelihood of conversions.

Furthermore, visual search can significantly impact marketing strategies. By optimizing product images and ensuring they are easily discoverable through visual search engines, businesses can drive more organic traffic to their websites. Additionally, visual search technology can be integrated into mobile apps, making it easier for users to search for products on the go.

In conclusion, augmented reality and visual search are revolutionizing the marketing landscape. By incorporating these technologies into their strategies, businesses can create immersive experiences, improve customer engagement, and drive more conversions. As technology continues to advance, mastering augmented reality and visual search will become paramount for marketers looking to stay ahead in the ever-evolving digital world.

Blockchain and Search Engine Marketing

In recent years, blockchain technology has emerged as a revolutionary force across various industries. While its association with cryptocurrencies such as Bitcoin has garnered significant attention, its potential extends far beyond digital currencies. One area where blockchain is poised to make a profound impact is in search engine marketing.

Search engine marketing (SEM) encompasses strategies and techniques aimed at increasing a website's visibility and driving targeted traffic through search engines. It involves both search engine optimization (SEO) and pay-per-click (PPC) advertising. With the integration of blockchain technology, SEM stands to undergo a significant transformation, unlocking new possibilities and addressing existing challenges.

One of the primary challenges in SEM is the lack of transparency and trust in advertising data. Advertisers often face issues such as click fraud, where fake clicks inflate advertising costs without generating any meaningful results. Blockchain offers a solution by providing an immutable and transparent ledger that records each click or ad interaction, ensuring that the data cannot be manipulated or tampered with. This transparency instills confidence in advertisers, allowing them to make informed decisions based on accurate data.

Moreover, blockchain's decentralized nature eliminates the need for intermediaries, such as ad networks or agencies, which can increase costs and create inefficiencies. By leveraging smart contracts, advertisers can directly connect with publishers, eliminating unnecessary middlemen and reducing transaction costs. This direct interaction also enables advertisers to have better control over their campaigns, ensuring that their ads are placed on relevant websites and reaching the intended audience.

Another crucial aspect of blockchain in SEM is the integration of microtransactions and tokenization. Blockchain enables the creation of digital tokens that can be used as a form of payment within the advertising ecosystem. This allows for more efficient and transparent transactions, eliminating the need for complex financial processes and reducing transaction fees. Additionally, the use of tokens can incentivize users to engage with ads, as they can be rewarded for their attention or actions. This creates a more engaging and mutually beneficial advertising experience.

In conclusion, the integration of blockchain technology holds immense potential for revolutionizing search engine marketing. Its ability to provide transparency, eliminate intermediaries, and enable efficient microtransactions and tokenization can address the challenges faced by advertisers and enhance the effectiveness of SEM campaigns. As the technology continues to evolve, marketers must stay informed and adapt their strategies to leverage the power of blockchain in their search engine marketing efforts.

Chapter 13: Ethical Considerations in Search Engine Marketing

Adherence to Search Engine Guidelines

In the ever-evolving world of digital marketing, understanding and adhering to search engine guidelines is crucial for achieving successful marketing effects. Search engines have become the gatekeepers of the online world, dictating how websites are ranked, indexed, and ultimately, discovered by users. As such, mastering these guidelines is essential for everyone involved in marketing efforts.

Search engine guidelines are a set of rules and best practices provided by search engines like Google, Bing, and Yahoo. They outline the dos and don'ts of optimizing websites for search engine visibility. By following these guidelines, marketers can ensure that their websites are search engine-friendly, improving their chances of ranking higher in search results and attracting organic traffic.

The primary search engine guideline revolves around creating high-quality, user-centric content. Search engines prioritize websites that provide valuable, relevant, and engaging content to their users. This means marketers should focus on producing informative articles, blog posts, videos, and infographics that address the needs and interests of their target audience. By doing so, they not only meet search engine criteria but also enhance the overall user experience.

Another important guideline is the proper use of keywords. Keywords are the words or phrases that users enter into search engines when looking for specific information. Marketers need to conduct thorough keyword research to identify the most relevant and popular keywords in their niche. They should then strategically incorporate these keywords into their website's content, meta tags, headings, and URLs. However, it's crucial to avoid keyword stuffing, a practice frowned upon by search engines that involves overusing keywords in an unnatural manner.

Furthermore, search engines value websites that are well-structured and easily navigable. Marketers should ensure that their websites have clear and intuitive navigation menus, allowing users and search engine crawlers to find and access all relevant pages easily. Additionally, optimizing website loading speed, using descriptive image alt tags, and creating mobile-friendly versions are also essential for adhering to search engine guidelines.

By adhering to search engine guidelines, marketers can lay a solid foundation for their online marketing efforts. Not only do they improve their websites' visibility and ranking in search results, but they also enhance the overall user experience. It's important to stay updated with any changes or updates to these guidelines as search engines regularly refine their algorithms to provide the best results to users.

In conclusion, adherence to search engine guidelines is vital for everyone involved in marketing effects. By creating high-quality content, utilizing keywords effectively, and ensuring website usability, marketers can improve their search engine visibility and attract organic traffic. Mastering these guidelines will enable marketers to stay ahead in the competitive world of search engine marketing.

Transparency in Advertising

In today's digital age, advertising has become an integral part of our daily lives. We are constantly bombarded with ads on various platforms, from social media to search engines. However, with the increasing prevalence of targeted advertising, concerns about transparency have also risen. Consumers are demanding more openness and honesty from advertisers, and this has led to a shift towards transparency in the advertising industry.

Transparency in advertising refers to the practice of providing clear and accurate information to consumers regarding the nature of the advertisement. It involves being upfront about the intent of the ad, the data collection practices involved, and the overall impact of the advertisement on consumers. This subchapter will explore the importance of transparency in advertising and its effects on marketing.

One of the main reasons why transparency in advertising is crucial is because it builds trust with consumers. In a world where privacy concerns are high, people want to know how their data is being used and why they are being targeted with specific ads. By being transparent about data collection practices and providing clear opt-out options, advertisers can foster a sense of trust and respect among their target audience.

Transparency also has a significant impact on the effectiveness of marketing campaigns. When consumers are aware of the intentions behind an advertisement, they are more likely to engage with it and make informed decisions. By providing accurate information and avoiding misleading claims, advertisers can create a positive brand image and establish long-term relationships with their customers.

Moreover, transparency in advertising helps to level the playing field for smaller businesses. In the past, larger companies with bigger advertising budgets had an advantage in reaching their target audience. However, with the rise of transparency, smaller businesses can now compete on a more equal footing. By being open about their products and services, smaller businesses can attract customers who value honesty and authenticity.

In conclusion, transparency in advertising is a vital aspect of modern marketing. It not only builds trust and credibility with consumers but also enhances the effectiveness of marketing campaigns. By being transparent about data collection practices, intentions, and the impact of advertisements, advertisers can foster positive relationships with their target audience. Moreover, transparency helps to level the playing field and allows smaller businesses to compete with larger corporations. As the demand for transparency continues to grow, advertisers must embrace this shift and prioritize honesty and openness in their advertising efforts.

User Privacy and Data Protection

In today's digital age, where technology plays a significant role in every aspect of our lives, user privacy and data protection have become paramount concerns. As marketers, it is essential to understand the impact our strategies can have on user privacy and take steps to ensure data protection. This subchapter will delve into the importance of user privacy, the implications of data breaches, and the steps marketers can take to safeguard user information.

User privacy is a fundamental right that must be respected. With the increasing amount of personal information shared online, users expect their data to be handled responsibly and securely. Failing to do so can have severe consequences on a brand's reputation and customer trust. Therefore, marketers must prioritize data protection and establish robust security measures to protect user information from unauthorized access and misuse.

Data breaches have become alarmingly common, with cybercriminals constantly finding new ways to exploit vulnerabilities. The consequences of a data breach can be devastating, not only for the affected users but also for the company responsible. Not only can it result in financial losses, but it can also lead to legal repercussions and damage to the company's brand image.

To safeguard user privacy and protect against data breaches, marketers must adopt best practices for data protection. This includes implementing secure data storage systems, using encryption technologies, and regularly updating security protocols. It is crucial to educate employees about the importance of data protection and ensure they adhere to strict privacy guidelines.

Transparency is also key when it comes to user privacy. Marketers should provide clear and concise privacy policies, outlining how user data will be collected, stored, and used. Obtaining explicit consent from users before collecting their data is vital, and they should be given the option to opt out if they wish.

In addition to these measures, marketers must stay updated with privacy regulations and comply with them. Laws such as the General Data Protection Regulation (GDPR) have been enacted to protect user privacy and impose strict penalties for non-compliance. By familiarizing themselves with these regulations and following the necessary guidelines, marketers can ensure they operate within legal boundaries and maintain trust with their audience.

In conclusion, user privacy and data protection are of utmost importance in today's digital landscape. Marketers must prioritize these concerns and take necessary steps to safeguard user information. By implementing robust security measures, being transparent with users, and complying with privacy regulations, marketers can build trust, protect their brand image, and mitigate the risks of data breaches.

Ethical Link Building Practices

In the vast world of search engine marketing, link building plays a crucial role in determining the visibility and credibility of a website. However, it is essential to adopt ethical practices when it comes to building links, as unethical methods can lead to severe consequences, including penalties from search engines.

Ethical link building practices revolve around the idea of acquiring high-quality links that provide value to both users and search engines. These practices not only help in improving search engine rankings but also contribute to long-term success in digital marketing efforts.

One of the primary ethical link building practices is creating valuable and engaging content. When your website offers informative and relevant content, it naturally attracts organic links from other sources. By focusing on creating high-quality content, you not only establish yourself as an authority in your niche but also encourage others to link back to your website.

Another ethical practice is guest blogging. This process involves writing and publishing articles on external websites that allow guest contributions. By showcasing your expertise and knowledge in your field, you can not only gain exposure but also secure valuable backlinks to your website. However, it is important to approach guest blogging with integrity and prioritize quality over quantity. Ensure that your guest posts are well-researched, well-written, and provide genuine value to readers.

Additionally, building relationships with other website owners and influencers is a key ethical practice. Engaging with individuals in your industry through networking events, social media platforms, and online forums can open doors for collaboration and link-building opportunities. By establishing genuine connections, you can build relationships based on trust and mutual benefit, leading to the acquisition of organic and high-quality backlinks.

It is crucial to avoid unethical practices such as buying links or participating in link schemes. These practices are not only against search engine guidelines but can also harm your website's reputation and rankings. Instead, focus on building natural links through ethical means, which will contribute to long-term success in your marketing efforts.

In conclusion, ethical link building practices are essential for any marketer looking to improve their website's visibility and credibility. By creating valuable content, engaging in guest blogging, and building genuine relationships, you can attract high-quality links that benefit both users and search engines. Embracing ethical practices will not only lead to improved search engine rankings but also establish your brand as a trustworthy and authoritative source in your niche.

Responsible Use of AI in SEM

In recent years, the field of search engine marketing (SEM) has witnessed a significant transformation with the emergence of artificial intelligence (AI) technologies. These advancements have revolutionized the way marketers approach their advertising campaigns, enabling them to make data-driven decisions and optimize their strategies for better results. However, with great power comes great responsibility. It is crucial for marketers to understand and embrace the responsible use of AI in SEM to ensure ethical practices and minimize any adverse marketing effects.

One of the key aspects of responsible AI usage in SEM is transparency. As marketers leverage AI algorithms to automate their campaigns and decision-making processes, it is essential to be transparent about the role of AI in their strategies. This means clearly communicating to the audience that AI is being utilized and how it influences the ad targeting and delivery. By doing so, marketers can build trust and foster transparency with their customers, helping them understand how their data is being used and empowering them to make informed decisions.

Another important consideration is the ethical collection and usage of data. AI-powered SEM heavily relies on data to deliver personalized and targeted ads. Marketers must ensure that the data they collect is obtained legally and ethically, respecting user privacy and adhering to data protection regulations. Additionally, they should prioritize data security and implement robust measures to safeguard sensitive information from unauthorized access or breaches, thereby safeguarding the privacy of their customers.

Moreover, marketers should be cautious about potential bias in AI algorithms. AI systems learn from historical data to make predictions and decisions, but if the training data contains biases, it can lead to discriminatory outcomes. It is essential to regularly audit and monitor AI algorithms to identify and mitigate any biases that may arise. By taking proactive steps to eliminate bias, marketers can ensure fair and equitable ad targeting, avoiding any marketing effects that may alienate or discriminate against certain groups of people.

Lastly, continuous monitoring and evaluation of AI-driven SEM campaigns are vital. Marketers should regularly assess the performance of their AI algorithms to ensure they are delivering the desired results and aligning with their marketing objectives. By closely monitoring campaign metrics and making necessary adjustments, marketers can optimize their strategies and mitigate any potential negative marketing effects that may arise from AI usage.

In conclusion, the responsible use of AI in SEM is of utmost importance to ensure ethical practices and minimize any adverse marketing effects. Transparency, ethical data collection, bias mitigation, and continuous monitoring are key pillars to achieve responsible AI usage. By adhering to these principles, marketers can harness the power of AI technologies in SEM while maintaining trust, fairness, and effectiveness in their advertising campaigns.

Chapter 14: Conclusion and Action Plan

Recap of Key Concepts

As we reach the end of this comprehensive guide on mastering search engine marketing, it is essential to recap the key concepts that we have covered throughout this book. These concepts will serve as a solid foundation for understanding and implementing effective marketing strategies using search engines.

Search engine marketing (SEM) refers to the practice of utilizing search engines, such as Google, Bing, and Yahoo, to promote businesses, products, or services. It involves both search engine optimization (SEO) and paid advertising methods like pay-per-click (PPC) campaigns.

One of the fundamental concepts to grasp is the importance of keywords. Keywords are the terms or phrases that users enter into search engines when looking for information or products. By conducting thorough keyword research, marketers can identify the most relevant and high-traffic keywords to optimize their websites or create targeted PPC campaigns.

Another crucial aspect to consider is on-page optimization. This includes optimizing meta tags, headings, URLs, and content to make it more search engine-friendly. By ensuring that your website is properly optimized, search engines will be able to understand its relevance to specific search queries, increasing the chances of higher rankings on search engine results pages (SERPs).

Off-page optimization is equally vital for a successful SEM strategy. This involves building high-quality backlinks from reputable websites, as search engines consider these links as a vote of confidence for your website's authority. Effective link building can improve your website's visibility and increase organic traffic.

Paid advertising methods like PPC campaigns are also key components of SEM. These campaigns allow marketers to bid on specific keywords and display their ads prominently on search engine results pages. By carefully managing these campaigns and monitoring their performance, marketers can drive targeted traffic to their websites and achieve higher conversion rates.

Furthermore, understanding the importance of analytics and tracking is crucial in evaluating the effectiveness of your SEM efforts. Tools like Google Analytics provide valuable insights into website traffic, user behavior, and conversion rates. By analyzing this data, marketers can make informed decisions, optimize their strategies, and achieve better marketing effects.

In conclusion, mastering search engine marketing requires a deep understanding of key concepts such as keyword research, on-page and off-page optimization, paid advertising methods, and analytics. By leveraging these concepts effectively, marketers can enhance their online presence, increase brand visibility, and drive relevant traffic to their websites. Whether you are a business owner, marketing professional, or simply someone interested in expanding their knowledge, mastering search engine marketing is an essential skill for achieving marketing effects in today's digital landscape.

Developing a Search Engine Marketing Strategy

In today's digital age, an effective search engine marketing (SEM) strategy is crucial for businesses of all sizes. With the ever-increasing competition in the online marketplace, having a strong presence in search engine results is essential for driving traffic, increasing brand visibility, and ultimately, achieving marketing success. This subchapter will guide you through the process of developing a comprehensive SEM strategy that will maximize your marketing efforts and yield tangible results.

To begin with, it is important to understand the core components of an SEM strategy. These include keyword research, ad creation, landing page optimization, and performance tracking. Keyword research involves identifying the specific search terms and phrases that your target audience is likely to use when searching for products or services similar to yours. This research will help you select the most relevant keywords for your SEM campaigns and optimize your content accordingly.

Once you have identified your keywords, the next step is to create compelling ads that will capture the attention of your target audience. These ads should be highly relevant, engaging, and persuasive, enticing users to click through to your website. Additionally, your landing pages should be optimized to ensure a seamless user experience and encourage conversions. This involves designing easy-to-navigate, visually appealing pages with clear calls-to-action and relevant content.

Tracking the performance of your SEM campaigns is crucial for understanding what works and what doesn't. By analyzing metrics such as click-through rates, conversion rates, and return on investment, you can make data-driven decisions and continuously refine your strategy to achieve optimal results. Regular monitoring and adjustments are essential to stay ahead of the competition and ensure the long-term success of your SEM efforts.

In addition to the technical aspects, it is also important to consider the broader marketing effects of your SEM strategy. A well-executed SEM campaign can not only drive traffic and increase conversions but also enhance brand awareness and credibility. By appearing prominently in search engine results, you establish yourself as a reputable and reliable source, which can lead to repeat business and positive word-of-mouth.

In conclusion, developing a search engine marketing strategy is a vital component of any comprehensive marketing plan. By conducting thorough keyword research, creating compelling ads, optimizing landing pages, and tracking performance, you can maximize your marketing efforts and achieve tangible results. Additionally, by considering the broader marketing effects of your SEM strategy, you can enhance your brand's visibility and credibility in the online marketplace.

Implementing and Monitoring the Strategy

Once you have developed a comprehensive search engine marketing strategy, the next crucial step is implementing and monitoring its effectiveness. In this subchapter, we will delve into the various aspects of executing your strategy and measuring its impact on your marketing efforts. Whether you are a marketing professional, an entrepreneur, or a small business owner, this section will equip you with the knowledge and tools necessary to maximize your marketing effects.

To begin with, implementing your search engine marketing strategy requires careful planning and coordination. You need to ensure that all elements of your strategy, such as keyword optimization, content creation, and website optimization, are executed seamlessly. This involves working closely with your team, whether it be in-house or outsourced, to allocate resources, set deadlines, and establish clear communication channels.

Once your strategy is implemented, it is essential to monitor its effectiveness. This involves tracking key performance indicators (KPIs) and analyzing data to measure the impact of your marketing efforts. By regularly monitoring your strategy, you can identify areas of improvement, adapt to changing market trends, and make data-driven decisions to enhance your marketing effects.

One of the essential tools for monitoring your strategy is web analytics. This powerful tool allows you to gather data on website traffic, user behavior, and conversions. By analyzing this data, you can gain insights into how well your strategy is performing, identify the sources of your website traffic, and determine which keywords and content are driving the most conversions. Web analytics also provide valuable information about user demographics, allowing you to tailor your marketing efforts to specific target audiences.

In addition to web analytics, social media monitoring is another crucial aspect of monitoring your strategy. Social media platforms provide valuable insights into customer sentiment, brand perception, and the effectiveness of your marketing campaigns. By monitoring social media mentions, comments, and engagement, you can gauge how well your strategy resonates with your audience and make necessary adjustments to improve your marketing effects.

Implementing and monitoring your search engine marketing strategy is an ongoing process. It requires continuous analysis, optimization, and adaptation to ensure that your efforts align with your marketing objectives. By implementing the right tools and regularly monitoring your strategy's effectiveness, you can maximize your marketing effects and stay ahead in the competitive landscape of search engine marketing.

Constant Learning and Adaptation

In the rapidly evolving world of search engine marketing, one thing is certain - the only constant is change. As search engines continually update their algorithms and user behavior shifts, marketers must stay on top of the latest trends and techniques to ensure their campaigns are effective.

This subchapter is dedicated to the concept of constant learning and adaptation in search engine marketing. It highlights the importance of staying abreast of industry changes and offers practical strategies for marketers of all levels.

First and foremost, it is crucial to understand that search engines are constantly refining their algorithms to provide users with the most relevant and high-quality results. What worked in the past may not yield the same results today. Therefore, marketers must be committed to ongoing education and staying updated on the latest best practices.

One of the most effective ways to stay informed is by following industry blogs, attending conferences, and participating in online forums. These platforms provide valuable insights from industry experts and allow marketers to network with peers facing similar challenges. By actively engaging in these communities, marketers can gain valuable knowledge and stay ahead of the curve.

Additionally, experimenting with new strategies and techniques is essential for mastering search engine marketing. A marketer should not be afraid to step out of their comfort zone and try new approaches. This can include testing different keywords, ad formats, landing page designs, or even experimenting with emerging technologies like voice search or artificial intelligence.

Furthermore, analytics play a vital role in the learning and adaptation process. Regularly analyzing campaign performance and user behavior data can uncover valuable insights that inform optimization efforts. By monitoring metrics such as click-through rates, conversion rates, and bounce rates, marketers can identify areas for improvement and make data-driven decisions.

Lastly, it is important to foster a culture of continuous learning within marketing teams. Encouraging team members to pursue certifications, attend workshops, or engage in professional development opportunities will ensure that everyone is equipped with the latest knowledge and skills.

In conclusion, mastering search engine marketing requires a commitment to constant learning and adaptation. By staying informed, experimenting with new strategies, leveraging analytics, and fostering a culture of continuous learning, marketers can effectively navigate the ever-changing landscape of search engine marketing and deliver impactful results for their organizations.

Resources for Further Exploration

In the rapidly evolving field of search engine marketing, it is essential to stay updated with the latest trends and techniques to maximize marketing effects. As a comprehensive guide for everyone, "Mastering Search Engine Marketing" provides an overview of the fundamental concepts and strategies to succeed in this dynamic landscape. However, to truly excel and harness the power of search engine marketing, it is crucial to explore additional resources that can further enhance your knowledge and skills.

1. Online Communities and Forums: Engaging with like-minded professionals can be an excellent way to exchange ideas, seek advice, and stay informed about the latest industry developments. Joining online communities and forums, such as Moz Q&A, Warrior Forum, or Reddit's /r/SEO, can provide valuable insights and foster connections with experts in the field.

2. Blogs and Newsletters: Many industry experts and thought leaders regularly share their expertise and insights through blogs and newsletters. Subscribing to popular marketing blogs, such as Search Engine Land, Search Engine Journal, or HubSpot's Marketing Blog, can keep you up-to-date with the latest trends, best practices, and case studies.

3. Webinars and Podcasts: Webinars and podcasts offer a convenient way to learn from industry experts without leaving the comfort of your own space. Platforms like SEMrush, Moz, and HubSpot frequently host webinars where you can gain in-depth knowledge about specific topics and interact with experts through Q&A sessions. Additionally,

podcasts like "Marketing School" by Neil Patel and Eric Siu or "The Digital Marketing Podcast" by Target Internet provide valuable insights and interviews with industry leaders.

4. Online Courses and Certifications: To gain a comprehensive understanding of search engine marketing and its various components, enrolling in online courses and certifications can be immensely beneficial. Platforms like Udemy, Coursera, and HubSpot Academy offer courses ranging from introductory to advanced levels, covering topics such as search engine optimization (SEO), pay-per-click (PPC) advertising, and analytics.

5. Industry Events and Conferences: Attending industry events and conferences can provide a platform for networking, learning from industry experts, and staying ahead of the curve. Prominent events like SMX, MozCon, and Pubcon bring together professionals from various niches of marketing effects, offering a wealth of knowledge through presentations, workshops, and networking opportunities.

By exploring these additional resources, you can continuously expand your knowledge base, stay informed about the latest trends, and enhance your skills in search engine marketing. Remember, the digital landscape is ever-evolving, and staying updated is the key to mastering this dynamic field.

www.ingramcontent.com/pod-product-compliance
Lightning Source LLC
LaVergne TN
LVHW021826060526
838201LV00058B/3521